The MYSTERY FANcier

Volume 9, Number 1
January/February 1987

The Mystery Fancier

Volume 8, Number 1
January/February 1987

TABLE OF CONTENTS

The Mystery Fancier
(USPS: 428–590)
is edited and published by-monthly by
Guy M. Townsend
1711 Clifty Drive
Madison, IN   47250

SUBSCRIPTION RATES: Second-class mail, U.S. and Canada, $15.00
per year (6 issues); first-class mail, U.S. and Canada, $18.00;
overseas surface mail, $15.00; overseas air mail, $21.00.   Overseas
subscribers please pay in international money order, check drawn
on U.S. bank, or currency; no checks drawn on foreign banks,
please.

Single copy price: $3.00
Second-Class postage paid at Madison, Indiana
ISBN: 978-1-4344-3634-4

WILDSIDE PRESS

Mysteriously Speaking ...

There's a good deal of news to report this time out, some of it good but some of it very bad indeed. The bad news is that we have lost two very talented and--what is more important--very decent people from our ranks: John Nieminski and Earl Bargainier.

JOHN NIEMINSKI

I first met John at the 1978 Bouchercon in Chicago, and the high point of every Bouchercon I have attended since then has been getting to spend some time with him and his good friend, Ely Liebow. Two finer people I never hope to meet, and now only one of them is left. I have asked Ely to write a piece on John for TMF and I hope to be able to present it to you soon. Those of you who knew John know what a wonderful person he was, and those of you who never met him have missed out on one of the rare unalloyed pleasures life has to offer. As I told Ely when I heard the news, as great a loss as John's death is to those of us who knew him, it is an even greater loss to those who never had--and now never will have--that pleasure.

A notice of John's passing was sent out by his associates at *Baker Street Miscellanea*, which I am going to take the liberty of quoting in its entirety:

> John Nieminski ("Abe Slaney," BSI) died of a heart attack at his Park Forest, Illinois, home on December 19, 1986. He was only fifty-seven years old, and his untimely death leaves his countless friends in Sherlockiana and mystery fandom bereaved.
>
> John had been a prominent member of Chicago's scion societies, The Hounds of the Baskerville (sic) and Hugo's Companions, for thirty-five years. He was a former Sir Hugo, a former editor of *The Grimpen Mire Gazette*, and the author of a detailed history of The Hounds, prepared in 1983 for the society's 40th anniversary. John was also active in DAPA-EM ("Elementary, my dear APA"), the mystery amateur press association for which he published his own newsletter, *Somewhere a Roscoe*, and he was a veteran of most of the seventeen Bouchercon mystery conventions to date, several of which he helped organize and run.
>
> After a long career as a U.S. Civil Service executive,

John had devoted himself in retirement to his favorite
literary pursuits. He loved Sherlock Holmes and mysteries
and English and American literature, and he loved research
about literature as much as the literature itself. He
shared his findings freely with others, and his *EQMM
350*, a guide to the first 350 issues of *Ellery Queen's
Mystery Magazine*, is almost legendary for its comprehen-
siveness and accuracy.

John was one of the founders of *Baker Street Miscellanea* in late 1974. Over the past twelve years, forty-
seven issues of BSM have been assembled under his en-
thusiastic editorship and loving eye for detail. BSM 47
was almost ready to go to press when John died. John
was the production editor responsible for BSM's technical
preparation, he handled unsolicited submissions, and he
also contributed many articles, editorial notes, reviews,
and puzzles to BSM. Even more, much of BSM's diversity
of Sherlockian and Doylean interests, and its good-natured
approach to the cultural phenomenon and its practitioners,
are due to John.

Most of all, John personified the spirit of good
comradeship in the Baker Street Irregulars. He enjoyed
nothing more than an opportunity to be with friends, and
they in turn will remember him for his irrepressible wit
and good humor. John will be missed tremendously.

We at *Baker Street Miscellanea* will miss John more
than most. From the outset, BSM has been a very personal
undertaking for all of us. John was a large part of the
remarkable personal chemistry that made editing and
publishing BSM a pleasure and a privilege for us. John
can never be simply replaced, and it is too soon to say
whether we will continue BSM without him. We must
now take stock of what is to be done, and we will inform
BSM's subscribers and contributors about BSM's future as
soon as possible.

EARL BARGAINNIER

I did not know Earl Bargainnier as well or for as long as I
knew John--I only saw him at a couple of PCA conventions, and
then only for short periods--but it was clear to me even on such a
brief acquaintance that he was one of life's gentlemen and gentle
men. He was an occasional contributor to these pages and we cor-
responded at irregular intervals down through the years. In fact, I
received a letter from him only a week or so before he died. At
the bottom of it is written, in pen, "Please don't publish any of
this drivel!" Earl never wrote a word of drivel in his life, and I
am going to take the liberty of disregarding his instructions in this
matter and sharing that letter with you. It is dated 19 December
1986, and it begins,

Dear Guy,
    I apologize for not having written earlier to tell
you how happy I am that TMF is back in business, and as
good as ever! One reason I have not written is that it
has been a busy fall semester for me; I have been on

seven committees and chairman of one (ironically, one to study faculty loads). The other reason is that I have had nothing to send you. I have had the research done for several months on an article to be called "Bernie Rhodenbarr: Lawrence Block's Burglar-Detective," but every time I plan to sit and write, something else comes up. However, when I finish it, I shall send it to you. I am getting tired of TAD. A year and a half ago I sent Mike an article on Lovejoy; it has yet to appear, and Gash has published two more since I wrote that article.

I was involved in a mystery symposium in Fitz-gerald, Georgia, in September, and there (so were George Dove and Jane Bakerman). It would take too long to explain why such a symposium took place, but I was paid nearly $1000 for participating. Unbelievable! Block said he had no plans to write any more Bernie books in the near future, and I hope he keeps his word. Margaret Ann Barnes (*Murder in Coweta County*) and Stuart Woods (*Chiefs*) were also at the symposium.

I shall try to have the article for your inspection by early spring.

All Best Wishes,
Earl

P.S. George Dove and I have a new book out: Cops and Constables: American and British Fictional Policemen.

Earl was a leading figure in the Popular Culture Association and especially in the PCA's Mystery/Detection Caucus, which sent out the following notice of his death:

It is our sad responsibility to tell you all of the unexpected death of Earl F. Bargainnier, Callaway Professor of English at Wesleyan College (Macon, Georgia). He died suddenly and peacefully in his sleep the night of January 3-4. We will all miss him both as a scholar and critic in our field and as a warm, supportive, generous person. Both the Mystery/Detection Caucus and the Popular Culture Association as a whole are diminished by his loss.

We are very much the poorer for the loss of these two very fine human beings.

THE SHORT SHEET

I have never been much of a fan of the short story. Outside of the Canon, I almost don't read them at all. But a good many of you people are not so limited and should rejoice to hear that Josh Pachter, himself an accomplished writer of short stories and editor of short story collections, has decided to convert the "Short Sheet" column he has been doing for *Mystery Scene* into a newsletter in its own right. In its new incarnation, *The Short Sheet* will contain reviews of short fiction in all of the mystery magazines as well as reviews of anthologies and short story collections by single authors. It will contain additional features as well. The newsletter will appear monthly (except where special double issues are involved), and the cost of a first class subscription is $20, which should be sent to:

4

Mysteriously Speaking ...

Josh Pachter, Erlangen Elementary School, APO NY 09066.

JOE L. HENSLEY

One thing that can happen when you work closely with someone is that you begin to take him for granted. It's not that you don't appreciate him; it just that you kind of blend into each other's lives. If you see a friend only once a year you may fall all over yourself greeting him, pumping his hand, embracing him, and telling him how great it is to see him again, but if you see that friend virtually every day, then a one-or-two-word greeting, a small wave of the hand, or even a brief nod may be all the greeting you exchange.

I don't know if I am peculiar in this, but I tend to compartmentalize my life. My job is a good example of what I mean. When you make your living, as I have for the past several years, dealing on a daily basis with burglars, thieves, drunk drivers and dope addicts, child molesters, the odd rapist and murderer, and other assorted villains, it's nice to be able to close the door tight on that compartment when you leave the office. *The Mystery Fancier* is another of my compartments, and when I sit down to work on putting together an issue my tendency is to close off the other compartments and concentrate on TMF. Now it happens that Joe Hensley has got a finger or a toe in several of the compartments of my life: I work with him, we have some peculiar family connections (you may read that however you wish), we share an interest in the mystery field and sometimes get involved in mystery projects together, and, most important, we are friends.

Most of you folks know Joe in only one of his numerous guises—as an accomplished and increasingly prolific mystery writer. Accordingly, when you are most likely to think of him or have him brought to your attention is when he has a new novel out or gets another short story published. That is only one aspect of the Joe Hensley I know, and in this case familiarity has bred forgetfulness. I have always made an effort to plug the successes of members of the TMF family, but I think that the last time I plugged anything Joe has written was in 1979, when *Minor Murders* (still my favorite Hensley novel) came out. He's averaged about a book a year since then, but I seem to have let them all get past me without comment. This year will see at least two and possibly three new books from him in print, and I have before me the dust jacket of the first of these—*Robak's Firm*, the second collection of Hensley short stories which Doubleday has published. (The first, *Final Doors*, was published in 1981 and contained some pretty remarkable stories. I've already mentioned that I'm no great fan of short stories, but several of the stories in this collection came close to converting me—"Paint Doctor," "Killer Scent," and "Lord Randy, My Son" are nothing short of masterful.) To get even a single collection of short stories published is quite a coup—look around you and you will see that single-author collections nowadays are only a shade less rare than hens' teeth—and to get a second volume published is a tremendous achievement in today's publishing market. The stories collected in *Robak's Firm* (Doubleday, $12.95) are every bit as strong as those found in *Final Doors*. Three of the stories, "Tourist," "Searcher," and "Finder," are related. Each is strong enough to stand on its own, but taken together they produce a whole that is greater than the sum of its

parts. "The Home" is a classy tale, too, but my favorite in the
bunch--indeed, my favorite Hensley short story to date--is "The
Retiree," which has the most satisfying ending I have read in many
a year. The highest compliment I can pay to a writer is entirely
involuntary--"Damn," I said to myself when I put down this story,
"I wish I had written that." Also due out this year is an updated
version of Joe's first novel, *The Color of Hate*. Walker is publishing
it under a different title--*Color Him Guilty*, I believe it is--which
is appropriate since Joe did a pretty complete rewrite on it. And
Joe has a brand new non-series novel (working title: *Fort's Law*) in
its final stages, which may be out toward year's end.
      This is good solid stuff, folks. If Ed Gorman's controversial
but quite accurate appraisal in *Mystery Scene* last year didn't send
you panting to the nearest book store, perhaps these remarks will.

GREENHILL CRIME CLASSICS

      I became an avid mystery fans when I was in my teens, and I
read voraciously (and indiscriminately) in the field for a decade and
a half before I discovered there was such a thing as mystery fandom.
I had read perhaps a thousand mysteries before I stumbled onto
TAD and had my eyes opened to the existence of critical works
about mysteries. I quickly acquired such works as I could lay my
hands on (and could afford)--Murch's *Development of the Detective
Novel*, reprints of Thompson's *Masters of Mystery* and Haycraft's
Murder for Pleasure, and Barzun and Taylor's *Catalogue of Crime*,
which arrived on the mystery scene about the same time that I did.
Through these works--and, though it is hard to believe in these
days when we are in danger of being overwhelmed by critical studies
of the mystery field, there were damned few other books to be had
on the subject at that time--I discovered that while I had, through
the catholicity of my readings, become fairly well grounded in
writers from the middle third of this century, there was a vast
world of earlier literature which I had not come across in my forays
into paperback book stores, supermarket magazine racks, and visits
to St. Vincent DePaul and the Salvation Army. Problem was, the
books I was reading about were already scarce, though their prices
had not yet skyrocketed through the roof, and it took me several
years of diligent searching and dealings with the few people who
were then selling mysteries by mail--speaking of whom, does anyone
know whatever happened to that splendid Evansville bookseller, Wilson
Campbell?--to come up with a fairly decent cross section of what
was being written in the field in the first three decades of this
century. Still, there were quite a few items that I lusted for for
years before finally giving up. Nowadays, what with the revival of
interest in mysteries and its attendant increase in respectability,
some of those books have again become available as reprints, and
that brings be at last to the point of this rambling discourse.
Israel Zangwill's *Big Bow Mystery* and Victor Whitechurch's *Crime
at Diana's Pool* were two of the titles that I never succeeded in
laying my hands on, but I have a copy of each before me as I type
this column, thanks to Lionel Leventhal of England's Greenhill
Books, which are distributed in this country by--are you ready for
this?--The Nautical & Aviation Publishing Company of America (101
West Read St., Suite 314, Baltimore, MD 21201). Also before me
are William LeQueux's *Count's Chauffeur* and George R. Sims' *Dorcas*

Deene, Detective. And soon to come, so I am assured by the boys at N&A, are Chesterton's *Club of Queer Trades,* Doyle's *Mystery of the Cloomber,* Fletcher's *Middle-Temple Murder,* and Wallace's *Nine Bears.* The books are of uniform size (5" x 8") and are uniformly bound in black cloth with gold stamping. They come with a handsome, gray dustjacket which features a likeness of Sherlock Holmes, complete with deerstalker and calabash. They appear in each case to be printed from the original plates, and the overall quality of the product is superior to the standard hardcover book which nowadays sells for anywhere from $12.95 to $15.95, which makes their price of $11.95 very attractive indeed.

CLIFFHANGER PRESS

Early this past January I received flyers from Cliffhanger Press (P.O. Box 29527, Oakland, CA 94604) announcing the publication of two new mysteries in a quality paperback format--*A Killing in Real Estate,* by Rudd Brown, and *Fly From Evil,* by Frank Free. At the top of one of the pages was a penned note from editor Nancy Chirich, saying that she would be happy to send review copies of these books to me if I wanted. Well, of course, I always want, so I wrote to her to say so--and my letter was returned to me by the Postal Service as "not deliverable as addressed--unable to forward." Now you folks know as much about this operation as I do.

NEW LETTERZINES

If you are a great fan of David and Maddie of *Moonlighting* fame--for my part I think that a) the series is rather silly and b) that whatshername just barely misses being homely, both of which opinions I realize place me in a distinct minority--then you may be pleased to learn that the TV series has inspired a letterzine, which goes by the name of *Once in a Blue Moon.* Issues are $1.50 per until the publication gets on its feet, at which time a regular subscription arrangement will be announced. Editor is Nicki Lynch, 4207 Davis Lane, Chattanooga, TN 37416.

Nicki is co-editor, with Sharon Rose, of a different letterzine, *A Suitable Job for a Woman,* which is "devoted to female mystery writers and female detectives." If you are interested in this one, send a buck-fifty to Sharon Rose, 203 Tally Road, Chattanooga, TN 37411. Both of these publications were still on the drawing board when I learned of them. The first issue of *Moon* was due out this March, with the first issue of *Job* to follow in April.

SHERLOCKON II

Given my tardiness in getting out this issue, this will probably be old news before you receive it, but I have received a flyer for this Sherlock Holmes convention, to be held 13-15 March at the Torrance Marriott Hotel in Torrance, California, and I am just passing it along FYI. Toastmaster: John Ball. Sherlockian Guest of Honor: Phyllis White. Professional Guest of Honor: Fred Saberhagen.

BEN SCHUTZ

Received the winter issue of Bantam's self-promo newsletter, *Deadline*, and there learned that Ben Schutz's first novel, *Embrace the Wolf*, is now out in paperback, and that his second novel, *All the Old Bargains*, will likewise be reissued between soft covers in April. That's good news for any of you who missed these when they came out in hardcover. Both are remarkably good, and *Embrace the Wolf* probably cost me a letter grade or two while I was in law school. It arrived in the mail one afternoon when I was supposed to be studying, and I made the mistake of reading the first couple of sentences before I put it on the shelf to be read after I graduated. I didn't get any studying at all done that day; I read the first chapter standing at the shelf, then I resigned myself to the inevitable and settled into a comfortable chair to finish it off. It was another "Damn--I wish I had written that" experience. The good news for those of you who have already read Ben's first two is that the third is due out from Tor in September, so Ben advised me on the phone this past weekend, and he is already working on number four. This guy does good work.

MURDER IN JAPAN

I had breakfast the last day of Bouchercon with John Apostolou (and a friend), and he told me about this item. I have since received this teaser, which I pass along to you unabridged: "Coming from Dembner Books (distributed by W.W. Norton) in Spring 1987: *Murder in Japan: Japanese Stories of Crime and Detection*, an anthology containing 14 short stories by 10 authors, edited by John L. Apostolou and Martin H. Greenberg, with a foreword by James Melville."

OTHER ITEMS

Cops and Constables: American and British Fictional Policemen, by George N. Dove and Earl F. Bargainnier, is published by Bowling Green State University Press, Bowling Green, Ohio 43403. It is available in paper or between hard covers. I regret to say that I don't have a price on either.

David R. Godine, Publisher (Horticulture Hall, 300 Massachusetts Avenue, Boston, MA 02115, has reprinted Fredric Brown's *Fabulous Clipjoint* in a trade paperback edition for $7.95.

One Garland release which I missed in my run-down an issue or two back--evidently it was out of print then but is now back in print--is *The Subject Is Murder: A Selective Subject Guide to Mystery Fiction*, by Albert J. Menendez. Menendez introduces each of the twenty-five subjects he covers (advertising, archaeology, the art world, etc.) with two or three brief paragraphs and then gets directly into the listings, which consist of author, title, place, publisher, and date. The main body of the book lists 3697 titles, and 115 additional titles are printed in an addendum. Included as an appendix is an eight page "Guide to Specialty Bookshops and Bookdealers." There is also an author index. If your are interested in reading mysteries about a particular subject--musical murders, for example, or mysteries involving department stores--there is absolutely no better place to start than this volume. I don't have a price for this extremely useful book, but its 332 pages probably put it in the $40 range. Garland's address is 136 Madison Ave., New York, NY 10016.

Lest it be thought that old Townsend is getting soft in his old age, let me savage briefly one of the latest releases from Writer's Digest Books--Barbara Norville's *Writing the Modern Mystery*, which you can purchase for $15.95, which is only about $15.37 more than it is worth. The dust jacket states that "mystery editor Barbara Norville" has been whipping the writings of the best and the brightest in the mystery field into shape for the past twenty years and more, and that "beginners and award-winners alike have profited from her problem-solving advice." Which is rather astonishing, given what I read in the first fourteen pages, after which I gave up. It is conceivable, I suppose, that starting on page 15 and continuing on without interruption until the end of the text on page 191, this creature is a model of lucid thinking, but I rather doubt it. On page 3 she dismisses the locked-room mystery with a contemptuous wave of her hand, saying that "contemporary authors, writing for a more sophisticated audience, have soft-pedaled the means of entry and exit.... At this writing I can think of only two authors who have used this purely cerebral exercise of howdunit, and then only in a modest way: Richard Forrest, in *A Child's Garden of Death*, and Orania Papazoglou, in *Sweet, Savage Death*." If I had an editor who revealed so superficial a familiarity with the mystery field as this astonishing comment reveals, I'd waste no time asking the publisher to assign me to someone else. That the locked-room or impossible crime elements have not been in the ascendancy for some decades is clear to everyone--but to say that there are only two contemporary author who have employed those elements, "and then only in a modest way," is just plain stupid, or arrogant, or both. I'd have to take off both shoes to be able to count all the times that just one contemporary writer--Bill Pronzini--has made use of those elements in his stories. To suggest that it has only been done twice in modern times is ridiculous.

And after I read the following paragraph at the top of page 5 I decided that Ms. Norville and I must be occupying different universes:

> In the literature of the past, the private eye was often a parody. He drank and wenched hard and consorted with seedy characters. His methods were not much different from those of the culprits he was tracking; he often worked outside the law. Since those early, crude days, the private eye has grown up. He has been given attributes that make him a more rounded, more interesting human being. He seldom has a wife but is either divorced or has a sometimes-live-in girlfriend. He is hardly ever promiscuous. He is literate, likes music, appreciates art and goes hunting and fishing. He dresses well but casually and knows his way around dessert spoons. He is often a college graduate. Sometimes he is an ex-cop, a background which provides either bitterness about his past or convenient contacts with old buddies still on the force.

It is clear from this that Ms. Norville has read Parker; apparently she subscribes to Parker's own view that it is therefore unnecessary to read anyone else.

"Chauvinism," as I have had occasion to mention in these pages more than once, means "vainglorious or exaggerated patriotism." It is true that a noisy bunch of ideologues, evidently lacking either the wit or the gumption to find words whose accepted meanings conveyed the ideas they were struggling to express, fell upon the perfectly respectable word chauvinist a couple of decades back, slapped a "male" in front of it and a "pig" behind it, and then paraded their poor, defiled victim around as though it were some wonderful thing that had fallen from the sky. But the fact that a flock of hysterical ninnies have tried to gang rape the word chauvinism is insufficient reason for thinking people and careful writers to abandon their standards. When I read these words at the beginning of a sentence on page 13, "Because the mystery field is still festooned with chauvinism ...," I felt a horrible, sinking feeling in my gut. Before finishing the sentence I considered the possibility that Ms. Norville was about to pursue the interesting line of thought that mystery fiction lends itself to the promotion of vainglorious or exaggerated patriotism, but my hopes were dashed when I returned to the page and read, "the heroine has been pretty much relegated to the genre of romantic suspense, with the muscular male coming in in the nick of time to save her from a fate worse than." [No, I didn't cut Ms. Norville off; she evidently likes to write cute incomplete sentences.] What are we to think of an editor, especially an editor who sets herself up as a teacher of those who would write well, who so egregiously misuses the English language? Had she used the expression "male chauvinism" in her sentence, her usage would have been comprehensible, if incorrect--just as the person who says "he don't" will be understood by his hearers despite his misuse of the language. But she used chauvinism unadorned, which seems to me to point inescapably to one of only two possible conclusions: first, that she has no idea whatever of the actual meaning of the word, in which case her knowledge of the language is so deficient as to render her incapable of teaching its usage to others; or second, that is aware of the actual meaning of the word but deliberately chooses to misuse it, in which case she is as unfit to teach writing as the lecher is to teach chastity.

Which brings up another point, which is that Ms. Norville seems to be as intent on preaching as she is on teaching. Witness her remarkable alternate universe remark that "In too many courts of law, a woman's alleged promiscuity is admissible evidence; a man's prior rape convictions are not" (p. 13), which is followed in the next paragraph by the suggestion that in writing story in which the rape victim avenges herself by killing the rapist, "Her satisfaction--and the reader's--in bringing the rapist to a kind of justice is enhanced by the pleasure of revenge against both the man and the legal system" (pp. 13-14). Revenge against the legal system? And with the haunting notes of the theme music from *The Twilight Zone* ringing in our ears, I leave you until the next issue--in which I promise to confine my ravings to far fewer pages than this.

Abandoned Queens
And Some Notes on Unintentional Plagiarism

Ola Strom

At the very end of *The Dragon's Teeth* (1939) we get the
following portrait of Mr. Ellery Queen receiving greetings from the
happy couple of his most recently closed case:

> But Mr. Queen only smiled vaguely and proceeded
> about his business, which was to worry himself to a
> shadow over another case.
> Which case?
> Well, that's another story

Mr. Queen just did not know how right he was. And how wrong.
He *was* to worry himself to a shadow over another case. But it did
not turn into another story. And that was the reason for the
worrying. You should always worry when the dog does nothing in
the nighttime. Then even Queens may be abandoned.

But this is starting in the middle of the story. Let us make a
hasty retreat to the beginning.

Detective fiction is primarily a literature of ideas and intrigue.
The novelty or individuality of a story lies first and foremost in
the twists of the plot: how a special crime originates and how it is
unravelled. Writing love stories you may use the same plot twice,
varying only the setting and descriptions, and get away with it.
This would be more difficult in mystery fiction, where the story
line is not in the same degree subordinate to descriptions and
atmosphere. Few things irritate addicts more than recognizing
well-used plots. This must be borne in mind also when an author
chooses to base a story on well-known motives used by other writers.
He had better have a new version of the plot; if he doesn't, the
readers will show little interest in his excuses.

As Ellery Queen, Frederick Dannay and Manfred B. Lee had
through the years begun writing several Ellery Queen mysteries
which for various reasons were never finished. Now, why should
we spend time on abandoned projects? If the authors themselves
were not satisfied with the result, why should others expect pleasure
from a reading? Well, the reason for abandoning a manuscript may
be that the idea does not work out as desired, but there may also
prove to be other reasons behind the abandonment, as we shall see
later.

We find a reference to an early abandoned novel in Jan Broberg's
1974 interview with Frederick Dannay:

I take care to interpolate that I have seen something
about Dannay and Lee having had notes for some other
detective novels in the thirties—one should have been
titled "The Swedish Match Mystery"—but Dannay waves
his hands:

"No indeed, but at that time we often received
letters with suggestions of enigmatic titles, and it is
possible that 'The Swedish Match Mystery' has been
among the suggestions.... On the other hand we have
had notes for a detective novel to be called 'The Indiana
Club Mystery,' but nothing became of it."[1]

The geographical adjective shows that the planning of "The
Indian Club Mystery" must have taken place in Queen's geographical
period, 1929-1936. Therefore it is quite interesting to find the
word "Indian" mentioned in the forewords to both *The Siamese
Twin Mystery* (1933) and *The Spanish Cape Mystery* (1935).

Nor is it a secret that Dannay and Lee had a new novel on
the way at the time of Lee's death in 1971. At first one got the
impression that the surviving partner in the team would finish it
singlehandedly:

Fred Dannay has announced that he will carry on with
Ellery Queen and has told me that most of the plot
outline of Ellery's next case had been worked out prior
to Lee's death. But his own poor health, his full-time
editorial and anthological duties, and the death of his
own wife in the summer of 1972 have resulted in a long
delay between novels. How much longer only time will
tell.[2]

In his interview with Broberg, Dannay appears rather pessimistic:

"Any new works under way?"
Frederick Dannay shakes his head, worried and
dejected: "There was a novel on the way when Manny
died—but during these years I have had so many other
problems. And there are not enough Queen short stories

---

[1]Jan Broberg, **Korsforhor: 12 deckarforfattare i vittnesbaset**
(Halmstad: Spektra, 1976), pp. 79–86, quotations from p. 85. It
appears that both persons involved have their memories playing
tricks on them. In the foreword to **Halfway House** (1936), Ellery
Queen points out that there is no reason why this book should not
have been called something like "The Swedish Match Mystery" (cf.
Francis M. Nevins, Jr., **Royal Bloodline: Ellery Queen, Author and
Detective** [Bowling Green, Ohio: Bowling Green University Popular
Press, 1974], p. 52). And yet, there is the best of reasons why
this novel could not bear that title. In Checkhov's collection entitled
The Cook's Wedding and Other Stories (1922) there is included a
story titled "The Swedish Match (The Story of a Crime)." Queen
had once been aware of this: compare his The Detective Short
Story (New York: Biblio and Tannen, 1969 [second printing]), p. 20.

[2]Nevins, **Royal Bloodline**, p. 211-212.

to suffice for a collection."[3]

And at last the coffin lid is closed: Nevins states that Dannay "gave up the idea of breaking in a new collaborator and writing more Ellery Queen novels, saying that it would be disloyal to Manny's memory"[4]—a view that appears a bit curious when we know the many cooperating teams behind the Queen books, from the novelizations of radio plays of the forties to the novels of the sixties, with Dannay backing up with Sturgeon and Davidson and Lee backing up with Vance, et al.

Any avid reader of Queen will eventually speculate on the empty years of Ellery Queen's authorship period. An author who in both the years 1932 and 1933 published no fewer than four novels a year, and the rest of the time in most years published at least one novel or collection, has a few conspicuous years in which no new work appeared: no new novels in 1940 or 1941; no new novels in 1946, 1947, or 1948; and the years between 1959 and 1962 are also empty. What is the reason for these gaps? Of course it may have been due to personal reasons, or work in other fields, and Nevins makes out a good case for *The Finishing Stroke* (1958) being planned as a swan song. But one always wonders of the author originally had plans for books that were somehow terminated. Queen researchers using this angle will stumble upon the fact that Queen is an exceptionally good example of one of the main difficulties of genre writing: the quest for originality.

Anybody hears about "simultaneous inspiration"? Or "Independent use of parallel ideas"? You discover that a book by one author uses the same gimmick as one written by another author. The former insists that he has never read or heard of the other book believed by some to be his model. The hardboiled among us may cry plagiarism, but he may be right: the world is so small and human imagination so limited that we may expect the same ideas to appear several times without this denoting wilful plagiarism.

Sometimes it is quite understandable that the author is ignorant of his or her predecessors. When Agatha Christie raised havoc with her Roger Ackroyd gambit in *The Murder of Roger Ackroyd* (1926), who was aware that the raconteur had been used as culprit already in the Norwegian *Jernvognen* (*The Iron Wagon*) by Stein Riverton in 1909? Or still earlier in Anton Chekhov's *The Tragedy of the Hunt* in Russian in 1884/85?[5]

Thus we may trace plot after plot and find that the author most famed for the use of a plot element is not necessarily the inventor: Kenneth Fearing's *The Big Clock* (1946) has a forerunner in Arthur Gask's *The Red Paste Murders* (1924), and Agatha Christie's courtroom trick in "Witness for the Prosecution" (in collection 1933) was foreshadowed in Frances Beeding's *Death Walks in Eastrepps*

---

[3]Broberg, Korsforhor, p. 86.

[4]Francis M. Nevins, Jr., and Ray Stanich, **The Sound of Detection: Ellery Queen's Adventures in Radio** (Madison, Indiana: Brownstone Books, 1983), p. 81.

[5]Bjorn Carling, **Norsk kriminallitteratur gjennom 150 ar** (Oslo: Gyldendal, 1975), p. 52.

(1931).⁶

The best known incidence may be the one told by Jan Broberg:

> Sometimes it may happen that a mystery author finds a
> plot that seems to him quite original. That was what
> happened to Nicholas Blake when he got the idea for "A
> penknife in my heart" 1958 (...), telling about how two
> men agree upon changing murders to avoid becoming
> suspects. When the novel was written Blake discovered
> that the American Patricia Highsmith had touched the
> same theme in her "Strangers on a train" 1950, by the
> way filmed by Alfred Hitchcock. But that was not enough!
> In 1961 Fredric Brown published his "The Murderers"
> with connections to both Highsmith and Blake.⁷

A more recent example involving quite reputable authors was discussed
in the Swedish magazine *Jury* 1979:4:52, where Nils Larsson compared
similarities in Ruth Rendell's *Make Death Love Me* and Margaret
Yorke's *Death on Account*, both published by Hutchinson in 1979.

Is it too much of a coincidence to believe all parties innocent
when two works with strong similarities appear practically at the
same time? That would be a case of one author talking about a
work in the writing and another stealing the idea, wouldn't it?
Not necessarily. People *do* get inspired with the same ideas simultaneously. It may be that they both read the same sources of
facts and figure out the same development. Or it may be "something
in the air." See this instance:

> Mallison (...) recalls Melville [Post] reading an interesting
> report of a trial in a newspaper and remarking that he
> would use it as the basis for a story. The two men then
> conversed at some length about the story, the journalist
> noted, and Post went so far as to present a potential
> plot he would employ, giving it immediately in some
> detail. Mallison tells that he waited expectantly for a
> period hoping to soon see the story published by some
> magazine, but to no avail. Somewhat later, on meeting
> Post again, he enquired about the progress of the story,
> and according to Mallison's recollection, the author replied,
>> I went down to Clarksburg yesterday and I
>> saw this month's *Cosmopolitan* in the window
>> of the newsstand, and on the cover I read, "In
>> this issue *The Mystery at the Thor Bridge* by
>> A. Conan Doyle," and I knew that Doyle had
>> beaten me to it. The funny part about it is
>> that the plot he built around the incident is
>> virtually the same as the one I had planned to

---

⁶See TAD 13:1:79, TAD 11:1:27, and John M. Reilly, ed., **Twentieth Century Crime and Mystery Writers**, second edition (New
York: St. Martin's, 1985), p. 59.

⁷Jan Broberg, **Mord for ro skull** (Malmo: Caverors, 1964), p. 220.

use.[8]

An experience of a lifetime, of course. Well, watch out and think
again.
    In the beginning of his career Ellery Queen was no trend-
setter, but a trend-capitalizer: at first he capitalized on the Van
Dine puzzle intrigues, and in the late thirties he threw more than
glances at the slicks. Then at last came the moment when he
evidently felt ready to experiment. Nevins reports the results:

> Queen had begun work on another novel, but the project
> ran aground halfway through its course when one of the
> cousins picked up a well-known national magazine and
> discovered that a new book by Agatha Christie being
> serialized therein, *And Then There Were None*, was based
> on exactly the same plotline. So it came about that
> there was no new Queen novel to open up the new decade
> [the forties].[9]

And Then There Were None, or more properly *Ten Little Niggers*
(1939), is quite famous for its plot: all residents on an isolated
island are killed one after another until all are dead and the killer
unknown even to the last remaining. One may easily understand
why Queen, relying on his surprising plots and intrigues, did not
want to follow in such footsteps.[10]
    This would be enough for one author, but as we know the
name Queen covered two persons and therefore ought to have more
in waiting. In an interview with Patricia McGerr we find this gem:
"I [once] met Ellery Queen (...), and he said that there were moments
when he almost wanted to murder me (...). You see, when my
[first] book was published he was halfway through writing a book
with exactly the same idea."[11] Now, McGerr's first, *Pick Your
Victim*, was published in 1946 and the problem of unveiling the
culprit is here substituted with the problem of finding the identity
of the victim. We may therefore conclude that also the second
lacuna in the Queen canon owes its existence to Queen finding
himself intercepted by another author.
    Of course this is hard on an author. But the ultimate problem
is the reader's: two Queen novels have been abandoned by the
author because their plots had too much resemblance to simultaneous
books by other writers. As one of the readers I personally feel
cheated. Fate has deprived me of two Ellery Queen novels based

[8]Charles A. Norton, **Melville Davisson Post: Man of Many
Mysteries** (Bowling Green, Ohio: Bowling Green University Popular
Press, 1973), p. 52. According to Hoch, in TAD 12:3:283, the inspir-
ation for these intrigues is Gross.

[9]Nevins, **Royal Bloodline**, pp. 63-64.

[10]On the other hand it should be noted that the Christie
novel is not the first of its kind either, as Barzun and Taylor tell
us in TAD 9:2:93, reviewing Bristow and Manning, **The Invisible
Host** (1930).

[11]Jan Broberg, **Mord i minne** (Goteberg: Zinedrman, 1976), p. 70.

on quite promising ideas by distributing the concepts too freely in
author circles.

And it is of course the fault of the readers, too. One reason
to give up such projects may be that the balloon has been pricked--
the first author marketing the idea gets to punch the audience in
the nose. A second punch is not that effective as the deliverer
meets a prepared receptor. But the second reason would frighten
any one, punch or no punch: what would a reader do upon reading
two stories published at nearly the same time and utilizing the
same plot skeleton? He would shout plagiarism and write damning
letters to the papers and publishers, that is what he would do.
And he would feel right about it, too.

I think that authors get the same ideas at the same time more
frequently than the readers may realize. The reason can be that
they consider the same events as fundament for fictional treatment
(cf. the Melville Davisson Post incident reported earlier). But ideas
also have their special time when they pop up in everyone's head;
different people make the same inventions simultaneously, so one
should be no more surprised when authors unbeknown to each other
toil at writing the same stories.

I believe that Richard Gordon once wrote an article describing
similar predicaments in mainstream fiction, a period when everyone
was writing books about that Knight of the Round Table Sir Lancelot
and Guinevere at the same time unaware of each other's common
interests.

Let us just observe how easily it happens: in her non-fiction
treatise on the writing of suspense fiction Patricia Highsmith has
described some of the inspirational background for her novel *A
Suspension of Mercy* (aka *The Story-Teller*) (1965):

> For months, maybe more than a year, I wanted to use a
> carpet as a means of concealment for a corpse, a carpet
> which someone carries in broad daylight, rolled up, out
> the front door of a house--ostensibly to the cleaners,
> while actually a corpse is inside it. I had not much
> doubt that this had been done. (...) Still, the idea in-
> terested me, and I tried to think how I could make the
> corpse-in-rug theme different and fresh and amusing.
> One obvious way was to have no corpse in it at all. In
> this case, the person carrying the carpet would have to
> be suspected of murder, would have to be seen carrying
> the carpet (perhaps in a furtive manner), would have to
> be a bit of a joker, in short. The germ was beginning
> to stir with life.[12]

Ms. Highsmith has tried to make an old idea seemingly fresh. Still,
she appears quite unaware that her new version had been used by
at least one other well-known mystery writer. You do remember,
don't you?[13]

But also Ms. Highsmith is aware of the general problem:

---

[12]Patricia Highsmith: **Plotting and Writing Suspense Fiction**
(second edition) (Boston: The Writer, 1972), pp. 5-6.

[13]Solution: by A.A. Fair [Erle Stanley Gardner], in **You Can
Die Laughing** (1957).

It has crossed my mind to write a suspense book from
the corpse's point of view. (...) But I am hardly original
in this idea. It has been used by more than half a dozen
crime novelists, according to the late Anthony Boucher,
and he adds, "It keeps recurring to people, always as a
new and striking idea."[14]

Anyone still believing that mere honesty on the author's part guar-
antees fresh ideas never used by others? Well-read authors may be
able to avoid plots that do not have the originality they seem to,
but if we expect the authors to read a sufficient number of books
to avoid stumbling they will not have time to write their own
works. This is a law of the awful cussedness of things in general
that readers have to accept.

The most impressionable way to demonstrate the fallacy of
accusing writers of plagiarism will be to remind you that even the
people unravelling plagiarism do plagiarize each other. In *The
Armchair Detective* in 1979 George Cloos pointed out the similarities
between two novels published in 1930 and 1931. Two years later
E.T. Guymon does exactly the same in the same journal.[15] Guymon's
information originates from a letter from one of the authors--neither
acknowledges the discovery by Cloos. Parallel inspiration, nearly
fifty years after--or what? See? You can't win.

So we must tolerate the fact that authors repeatedly get the
idea of pitting Sherlock Holmes against Jack the Ripper claiming to
create novelties each time. But in return it bugs me that I shall
never learn how Ellery Queen would have solved the *Ten Little
Niggers* case. It is a pity. I shall always wonder if Ellery was
meant to be murdered, too, to comply with the premise of the plot.

I suppose the Queens left no dying message on how to retrieve
and complete their manuscript notes?

---

[14]Highsmith, p. 83.

[15]See TAD 9:2:161 and 11:1:2. And, okay--the books are Don
Basil, **Cat and Feather** (1931) and Roger Scarlett, **The Back Bay
Murders** (1930)--constituting as it seems a real case of plagiarism.

Cornell Woolrich: The Last Years
Part III

Francis M. Nevins, Jr.

Nothing new by Woolrich appeared for the next three years, but that didn't stop him from trying to maintain the illusion that he was still an active writer. He sold the editors of the new hard-boiled mystery magazine *Manhunt* a story called "The Hunted" which he claimed was new, but when it was published in that periodical's January 1953 issue a long-memoried reader wrote in to point out that the tale had first appeared in the pulps fifteen years before as "Death in the Yoshiwara" (*Argosy*, 29 January 1938). Meanwhile Woolrich continued to rewrite and update old pulp stories for distribution to subscriber newspapers by King Features Syndicate, and a few at least of these retreads were published as new Woolrich thrillers.

Yet it is clear that Woolrich hadn't totally abandoned writing during the middle fifties. His typewriter time, such as it was, was devoted to his most ambitious mainstream project since his pre-crime fiction of the Fitzgerald era: an episodic novel about the birth, youth, prime, middle age, decline, and death of a New York hotel much like the ones in which he and his mother had spent so much of their lives, with each individual chapter taking place in the same room at a different moment in the building's lifespan. We know Woolrich was working on this project at least as early as 1955, since one of its episodes, the only one in fact that could be classified as a crime story, was published in a *Manhunt*-like magazine late that year ("The Black Bargain," *Justice*, January 1956). The other parts of the book-in-progress were of interest neither to genre magazines like EQMM nor to periodicals that ran mainstream fiction. Woolrich kept plugging away at the work as and when he could.

During the time when he was struggling with that project and with the domestic nightmare of his mother's worsening health, he contracted with the publishing house of Dodd Mead to do two collections of short stories. The understanding was that each of the books would contain two tales from previous collections, two older magazine stories not previously collected, and two thrillers never published before anywhere. Whether Woolrich ever intended to write four new stories for these books or was deceiving Dodd Mead all along is not known. In fact, he passed off revised versions of four old pulp stories as fresh from his typewriter, and the publisher advertised them as such.

Nightmare (Dodd Mead, 1956) opens with one of these allegedly new items, "I'll Take You Home, Kathleen," a haunting *noir* story about an ex-con who comes home to find his girl friend murdered and himself the target of a lunch mob. It had originally been published as "One Last Night" (*Street & Smith's Detective Story Magazine*, May 1940). This was followed by a Hollywood whodunit, "Screen Test," which was an updated and much poorer version of Woolrich's third published crime tale, "Preview of Death" (*Dime Detective*, 15 November 1934). The two stories culled from previous collections were those supreme classics of *noir* fiction, "Three O'Clock" (perhaps the finest story Woolrich ever wrote) and "Nightmare." The pair of old but hitherto uncollected tales chosen for the book were the powerful "I.O.U." and the workmanlike "Bequest." What needed to be said about the volume was, as usual, said best by Anthony Boucher in his review for the *Times*:

> By sober critical standards there is just about every-
> thing wrong with much of Woolrich's work. This collection
> of six stories illustrates most of the flaws: the "explanation"
> that is harder to believe than the original "impossibility,"
> the banal and over-obvious twist of "irony," the casual
> disregard of fact or probability (the Los Angeles Police
> Department so under-staffed that only a single investigator
> of low rank can be spared to handle the murder of a
> film star!). However, critical sobriety is out of the
> question so long as this master of terror-in-the-com-
> monplace exerts his spell. It is an oddly chosen collection,
> representing neither the best nor the least familiar of
> Woolrich..., but it is characteristic, and I do not envy
> the hard-headed reader who can resist its compulsive
> black magic."

If Woolrich's creative life in the mid-fifties had gone stale, his physical environment was in even worse shape. The Hotel Marseilles, which had been home to him and his mother since the worst days of the Depression, was turning into more of a dump each year as successive managements kept finding new corners to cut. The building's floors were coated with an "ingrained and ineradicable grime," the airshaft was filled with combustible debris, the fire stairs were littered with fruit peels and beer cans and pages from old newspapers. Every bulb had been stolen from the fire stairs walls, and going down those steps was like "running inside a box in the dark." Woolrich's description makes the place sound like one of those dreadful tenement buildings we see every week on *Hill Street Blues*. Near the end of his long tenancy there wasn't even a telephone connection between his apartment and the lobby, because in the latest economy move the downstairs switchboard had been taken out.

Over the years, his autobiographical manuscript tells us, "as the concentration camp of Harlem burst apart its barbed-wire bounda-ries," the Marseilles had filled up with blacks. By 1957 he and his mother were the only whites on their floor, and their neighbors included a prostitute, an alcoholic welfare mother, and some of the poorest of the working poor. He expressed no queasiness about his racial isolation; quite the contrary. "We were all just people together. Some poor, some better off than that; some young, some older than that; some healthy, some (like my mother) sick almost unto death."

Claire Woolrich had suffered a massive heart attack in the spring of 1956. Afterwards, although she could still move around freely within the apartment, she was unable to go outdoors. From then on her son was as surely a prisoner of the Marseilles as if a turnkey had locked him in each night. Why hadn't they left the place before then? The only rationale Woolrich offers in his auto-biography is the feeble excuse of habit. The building was "a home to us," he says. "We were used to it, and I felt with all a writer's typical superstition that it had brought me luck and it would have been ungrateful of me to move."

They were still living in that shabby cocoon as the summer of 1957 faded into fall. A few weeks later, on October 6, at the age of eighty-three, Claire Attalie Woolrich died. A service was held at the Walter B. Cooke Funeral Home, on West 72nd Street, and her body was interred in the family crypt at the Ferncliff Mausoleum, in Hartsdale. The day she died was the day he began his own long walk to the grave.

He wrote nothing for publication about his reaction to her death, and in his autobiography he dismisses the subject with four laconic words: "She is gone now...." If there were anyone to whom he could have spoken his feelings, he might have said what Raymond Chandler had written to two friends less than three years earlier about the death of his wife, who had been old enough to be his mother: "She was the music heard faintly at the edge of sound. It was my great and now useless regret that I never wrote anything really worth her attention, no book that I could dedicate to her.... She was the light of my life, my whole ambition. Anything else I did was jus the fire for her to warm her hands at."

Several years later, Woolrich said to science fiction writer Barry N. Malzberg: "Life is death. Death is in life. To hold your one true love in your arms and to see the skeleton she will become; to know that your love leads to death, that death is all there is, that is what I know and what I do not want to know and what I cannot bear." Whom could he have been speaking of, except his mother?

Her death had no effect on his diminished output as a writer, nor on his attempts to pretend he was as active as ever. Late in 1957, *Manhunt* offered another Woolrich story advertised as new, and once again the editors learned that they'd been scammed: "The Town Cried Murder" (*Manhunt*, January 1958) was a revised version of an old pulper, "The Hopeless Defense of Mrs. Dellford" (*Dime Detective*, December 1942). This time they took legal action against Woolrich and got their money back.

But the incident didn't teach him a lesson. In mid-1958 came *Violence* (Dodd Mead, 1958), the second and final of those Woolrich collections that were supposed to contain a sizeable proportion of brand-new stories. This time three out of the six tales in the book were old pulpers somewhat updated and passed off as new: "Murder, Obliquely" (originally "Death Escapes the Eye," *Shadow Mystery Magazine*, April-May 1947), "The Corpse in the Statute of Liberty" (originally "Red Liberty," *Dime Detective*, 1 July 1935), and "That New York Woman," which was the same rewrite of "The Hopeless Defense of Mrs. Dellford" that Woolrich had palmed off on *Manhunt* as a new story several months before. But the volume also revived two all-time Woolrich classics, "Don't Wait up for Me Tonight" (originally "Goodbye, New York," *Story Magazine*, October 1937) and "Guillotine." As a sort of makeweight, the editors threw in a condensation of the first part of Woolrich's 1952 fantasy-horror tale, "The Moon of Montezuma." Even Anthony Boucher was taken in by the false advertising about the collection, describing the tales in *Violence* as "all new to book form"--which "Guillotine" certainly

wasn't--and as including "some never published before anywhere."
But he wasn't overwhelmed by the choice of stories. Among the
six only "Guillotine", he commented, "ranks with the best of Woolrich's
unforgettable pulp classics ... but all of them display, if to a lesser
extent, his mastery of detail in creating tension and terror out of
the commonplace."
     In July of 1958, about a month after Dodd Mead released the
Violence collection, the prestigious firm of Random House published
its first and only Woolrich title, the episodic novel on which the
author had worked sporadically for years. *Hotel Room* was dedicated

To
Claire Attalie Woolrich
1874-1957
In Memoria
This Book: Our Book

and, except for one chapter, was completely devoid of crime elements;
but no other person in the world could have written a line of it.
The story of New York's Hotel St. Anselm--of its birth, adolescence,
maturity, old age, and death--and the stories of the people who
checked into Room 923 of that hotel at various points in the building's life, represents Woolrich's last attempt to break into the
mainstream and be accepted as a writer, not just as a suspense
writer. It failed. The book wasn't even review in the *Times* as
almost all of Woolrich's suspense novels and story collections had
been; it wasn't picked up by any of the book clubs or paperback
houses; it earned pitiful royalties for a few months; and then it
died. No one has seen fit to resurrect it since. The reasons for
its failure are understandable. Woolrich was straining mightily to
write a significant work, and the huffing and puffing showed on
the pages. The style is ponderous, overloaded to the point of
laughability with elephantine metaphors and similes, posturings and
preachments. *Hotel Room* reads as if Woolrich thought that the
vivid all-but-cinematic word magic that had invested his suspense
fiction was somehow the enemy of serious literature. His renunciation
of his most singular gifts produced a book that is often positively
painful to read. On the other hand, its structure and much of its
content are well within the boundaries of the dark universe he'd
been exploring for all his adult life.
     The book's opening chapter, "The Night of June 20, 1896,"
unfolds on the St. Anselm's first night in existence, which is also
the first night in the married life of Mr. and Mrs. John Compton.
The newlyweds check into Room 923 for their honeymoon, but John
steps out for a few minutes so that his bride can undress in privacy
and, like characters in some of Woolrich's best suspense stories--
"Finger of Doom," "You'll Never See Me Again"--almost literally
steps off the face of the earth. Unlike the vanishing people in
those stories, John never returns, and his disappearance turns his
wife into a catatonic. "Good-bye, Johnny! Good-bye!" she murmurs
as the story ends. "And good-bye to me too. For we both died in
here the other night."
     The next two chapters are two halves of a single story whose
plot and mood recall the knowing, worldly-wise tales Woolrich
wrote for magazines like *Smart Set* and *College Humor* back in the
twenties. On "The Night of April 6, 1917," a few hours after the
United States' entry into World War I, a shy and naive young man

checks into Room 923, having just enlisted in the army, and calls his favorite girl to invite her to a night on the town before he goes overseas. Ted and Jean end their night getting married in rural Connecticut at 4:00 a.m., and they make a date to meet in the same Room 923 and resume their relationship on the night the war ends. Don't ask how they could expect Ted to be back in the States a few hours after the guns fell silent; just remember this is a story of romantic naivete. As it happens, Ted *is* back on "The Night of November 11, 1918" and keeps his date, but in the year and a half since their wedding night both he and Jean and the nation as a whole have entered the twentieth century. The couple have not the least physical attraction to each other, and each has found new lovers, but they discover that they can still be the best of buddies, and the story ends with Ted offering to drive Jean to her date with a new boyfriend.

"The Night of February 17, 1924," which had been published in *Justice* as "The Black Bargain," is a Prohibition tale about the last hours of a doomed gangster. Woolrich spends many a page making Jake Abbazzia such a hateful creep we want to see him dead, but then when our wish becomes reality and Abbazzia is cornered by rival mobsters in Room 923, the gears are shifted and we are made to live the last moments of his life from his perspective and indeed to experience dying with him. In this sense the story belongs with Woolrich classics like "Three O'Clock" and "Guillotine" and proves that, even this late in his career, Woolrich could make us ache for the most depraved when they were face to face with nothingness.

The weakest and most perverse chapter in *Hotel Room* is "The Night of October 24, 1929," whose subject of course is the collapse of the stock market. Into Room 923 comes a ruined businessman who intends to settle his personal affairs that night and go out the window at dawn. Then, while poised on the ledge, he imagines the rising sun speaking to him with the voice of God, reminding him that the Almighty has set his canon 'gainst self-slaughter, chewing him out as a coward who can't take a little punishment--and sure enough the man decides to be a *real* man and live. Is the story a fossil from the Catholicism of Woolrich's youth? A sign that he feared and hated death so much that he couldn't conceive of any adequate reason to take one's own life? I suspect the answer to both questions is Yes. Is it a good story? No.

Next comes a very short and bleak chapter in which a young man named Ken checks into Room 923 with a young woman. They are desperately in love and have defied their respective parents to be together, but not only won't Ken have sex with her until they're married, he literally won't sleep in the same bed with her, and he asks the desk clerk to have a cot installed in the room for him. After a full dose of blissful thoughts about her future happiness with him, the woman drifts off into sleep, murmuring her beloved's name. Ken. Ken. *Kensuke Murakami.* Only then do we learn that the title of this chapter is "The Night of December 6, 1941."

Finally, on "The Night of September 30, 1957"--the last night before the St. Anselm is demolished to make way for an office tower--an ancient lady checks into the decrepit hotel, insists on staying in Room 923, slowly prepares herself for bed, and we just as slowly realize that she is the same Mrs. John Compton who slept in this room back in 1896. After thanking John for a perfect marriage--no shadows, no pain, no sickness or fear or strife--she dies in her sleep that night.

More than any other completed book of his late years except perhaps *Fright*, Woolrich in *Hotel Room* created a form in perfect harmony with the vision of a man who'd confined himself in one hotel room or another for almost all his adult life. The same claustrophobic setting crops up in so many of his final stories, both before and after *Hotel Room*'s publication, that it can fairly be called the last obsession of his career.

Briefly mentioning the book in his "Best Mysteries of the Month" column in the November 1958 EQMM, Anthony Boucher described *Hotel Room* as "less a novel than a collection of episodes, many with the impact of [Woolrich's] crime shorts." It would have been an even stronger volume if one chapter hadn't been removed from the book manuscript so that all of the *Hotel Room* episodes except its first and last would be tied, however loosely, to some historic American event. The excised chapter, which Woolrich called "A Penny for Your Thoughts," was bought by Fred Dannay for $250 and published in the September 1958 EQMM as "The Penny-a-Worder"—the first Woolrich original the magazine had ever run. The situation in the story may well have been autobiographical: sometime in the late 1930s, a struggling pulp crime writer named Dan Moody checks into Room 923, assigned to grind out a novelette literally overnight so as to match the previously commissioned cover artwork on a forthcoming issue of a *Dime Detective*-like magazine. Limiting himself not just to one setting but to one main character, Woolrich not only keeps us on the edge of our seats but gives us the most vivid evocation ever written of the insane pressures and feverish energy of the pulp writer's life, and he manages to make the fate of a hackneyed pulp thriller stand for the fate of all creative achievement in this sad old world.

Once the *Hotel Room* manuscript was delivered to Random House, Woolrich became momentarily interested in trying his hand at original scripts for television. He'd made a small fortune out of TV adaptation rights to his stories since as far back as 1946, but he was never able to sell the medium either of the teleplays he wrote twelve years later. This failure won't surprise anyone who has read his twin efforts. But he did manage to sell magazine publication rights to both plays within a short time after they were completed. Fred Dannay paid $250 for "Working Is for Fools," a sappy rewrite of the 1936 pulper "Dilemma of the Dead Lady" (better known as "Wardrobe Trunk"), and then sat on the manuscript for almost six years. Almost simultaneously Robert P. Mills, Tony Boucher's successor as editor of the prestigious *Magazine of Fantasy and Science Fiction*, offered Woolrich $150 for the occult play "Which Is You? Which Is I?" which he published as "Somebody's Clothes—Somebody's Life" (*The Magazine of Fantasy and Science Fiction*, December 1958). Outside the great casino at Biarritz, a countess, ruined by gambling fever and on the brink of suicide, suddenly finds herself inside the body of another woman, one who has in fact just jumped off a cliff into the sea. Then she discovers that in her new identity she's supporting her blind husband on her earnings as a prostitute. It's a bizarre tale with some genuine touches of *noir* amid the wild emotionalism, but no one would rate it among Woolrich's best and no one with a lick of sense would have put it on television then or now.

TO BE CONTINUED

The "I" in the Private Eye

V. Louise Saylor

The phrase "in the tradition of Hammett, Chandler and Macdonald" appears with great frequency in criticism, reviews and
promotional advertising for contemporary detective fiction.   For
those who are addicted to the genre, the words act as a Pavlovian
bell which recalls the characteristics generally associated with the
original hard-boiled private detectives: the lone, wise-cracking man
adhering to his own personal code in a corrupt, female-and-ac-
tion-packed, realistic, California setting.   The promise of a new
novel in the desired tradition attracts many readers' attention, and
it continues to do so even if the promise is not always fulfilled.

Assuming that all, or even most of, the basic characteristics
are fairly skillfully presented, what else should be in a book that
promises to continue in the tradition of Hammett, Chandler or
Macdonald?   For this reader, the detective must tell his--or her--
own story, as did the Continental Op, Philip Marlowe and Lew
Archer.   While the early tough-guy writers used the first-person
narrative in differing ways, the effect is the same.   The reader is
drawn into the suspenseful story and into the detective's world, for
"the very fact that we have before us ... an identifiable narrator
telling us the story directly ... imparts a tangible reality to the
narrative situation and a substantial veracity to the account we are
reading."[1]

HAMMETT AND THE CONTINENTAL OP

Sam Spade is the model hard-boiled private detective for many
genre fans.   But, because Hammett used the third person narrative
for *The Maltese Falcon*, these comments will focus on Hammett and
the Continental Op.

In a letter to Mrs. Knopf, Hammett remarked "Then I want to
try adapting the stream-of-consciousness method, conveniently
modified, to a detective story, carrying the reader along with the
detective,... letting the solution break on both of them together."[2]

---

[1]William Riggan, **Picaros, Madmen, Naifs, and Clowns: The
Unreliable First-Person Narrative** (Norman: University of Oklahoma
Press, 1981), pp. 18-19.

[2]William Marling, **Dashiell Hammett** (Boston: Twayne Publishers,
1983), p. 48.

Although the Op occasionally mentions a passage of time, such as "A week or two after this conversation," or "So, all in all, it was nearly eight years later,"[3] most of the tales appear to unfold before the reader as the events occur. The dialogue and the Op's narrative use of the present tense from time to time reinforce this sense.

In addition, the Continental Op's narration has a lean immediacy that is produced by active verbs and compact sentences. Hammett builds and sustains suspense through limited imagery, liberal use of dialogue, and suppression of the Op's feelings in the descriptive passages. As Peter Wolfe observes, Hammett "forgoes psychic depth to describe fast-moving action in well-drawn settings. Tension comes from the accuracy of detail and intensity of observation he lends to the building plot."[4]

Hammett is the only one of the three writers who does not show character development or allow the reader into the detective's mind; the relationship is kept on a polite, acquaintance-basis only level. Yet, the reader does get involved in the story in a number of ways. First: "Hammett doesn't narrate. Instead, he makes things happen to people. Then he makes us wonder where the excitement came from and what it meant." And second: "Hammett avoids giving insights into his characters' thoughts and feelings in order to compel greater reader participation."[5]

CHANDLER AND MARLOWE

However, when reading Chandler, the story line and action are almost secondary to the enjoyment of "knowing" Marlowe and being privy to his observations. In his published letters and critical writing, Chandler stated more than once that a character should be created rather than described. The emergence of the main character, the detective, through inference is most likely the most important facet of the first-person narrator/protagonist in the hard-boiled genre.

Marlowe tells his own story. The observations and descriptions are his—shaped by his world view, and presented in a way that the reader gains an understanding of Marlowe, and is enveloped by the world in which he lives. Marlowe is a very observing detective, and as Chandler was a writer of scenes, the visual impact on the reader is direct and unavoidable.

Hammett and Chandler have been credited with writing in, and even with creating, a vernacular that established the standard diction for the genre. But Chandler, and then to some extent Macdonald, employed what could be labeled—for want of a better term—a descriptive vernacular. That is, the narrator sets the fictional scenes and describes the other characters in a manner that forces a mental image for each reader. For instance, the reader is offered a complete picture with this line: "On the smooth brown hair was a hat that

[3]Dashiell Hammett, The Continental Op (New York: Random House, 1974), p. 164.

[4]Beams Falling: The Art of Dashiell Hammett (Bowling Green, Ohio: Bowling Green University Popular Press, 1980), p. 19.

[5]Ibid., pp. 18–19.

had been taken from its mother too young."[6] Even though each
reader will picture a different hat, the words evoke a picture of a
hat that would answer the description of having been taken from
its mother too young. Occasionally Chandler achieved this descriptive
force with the simile. The visual impact of this Chandler line is
undeniable: "A few locks of dry white hair clung to his scalp, like
wild flowers fighting for life on a bare rock."[7] But, the intensity
of the impact is underscored when the observation is contrasted
with another: "His head was partly bald; and a few strands of hair
lay lankly across the top of his scalp."[8] The latter, while not
Macdonald at his most colorful or poetic, is perfectly acceptable
prose; yet, the visual force does not compare.

Unfortunately, even with Chandler's skill, not all of Marlowe's
similes produce an immediate image, and the flow of the narrative,
and the reader's involvement with it, are interrupted. For example,
when Marlowe observes that some plants "smelled as overpowering
as boiling alcohol under a blanket,"[9] the reader has to stop and
search for what that meant to Marlowe—or could have meant to
Chandler.

In addition to vivid and compelling imagery, Marlowe's narrative
is laced with humor. For the protagonist to be created, for the
reader to become absorbed in the character, the wit must be the
protagonist's own. For instance, while coming out of a drugged
state, Marlowe muses on a possible news item:

> Philip Marlowe, 38, a private license operator of shady
> reputation, was apprehended by police last night while
> crawling through the Ballona Storm Drain with a grand
> piano on his back...Asked why he was wearing spurs
> Marlowe declared that a client's confidence was sacred."[10]

Thus, the reader learns about Marlowe through his self-deprecating
humor and seemingly endless wisecracks—those outlets that enable
him to persevere.

An additional facet of Marlowe's personality emerges with
lines such as: "There are days like that. Everybody you meet is a
dope. You begin to look at yourself in the glass and wonder."[11]
The veracity of the first-person narrative allows the reader to
comprehend, and believe, the many comments that emphasize and
reinforce Marlowe's solitary condition.

Although Marlowe does not always relate events as they occur,

---

[6]Raymond Chandler, **The Little Sister** (New York: Ballantine
Books, 1971), p. 4.

[7]Raymond Chandler, **The Big Sleep** (New York: A.A. Knopf,
1966), p. 6.

[8]Ross MacDonald, **The Galton Case** (New York: Bantam Books,
1960), p. 6.

[9]**The Big Sleep**, p. 5.

[10]**The Little Sister**, p. 165.

[11]Ibid., p. 51.

there are few intrusive "had I but known"-type comments. Yet, in
the evolution of the hard-boiled tradition, the immediacy of Hammett's
style is softened by Marlowe's reflections and personally shaped
descriptions.   But, that loss of immediacy is offset with a more
fully realized protagonist. As Ross Macdonald once observed: "Chandler's novels focus in his hero's sensibility, and could almost be
described as novels of sensibility."[12]

MACDONALD AND ARCHER

As with the stories which feature the Continental Op and
Marlowe, and for many of the same reasons, the reader becomes
involved in an Archer novel--if only by maintaining a genealogy
tree as the veneer peels away from the complex multi-layered relationships portrayed therein.
To state that the Archer novels of Ross Macdonald changed
over the years is not an original observation. Many critics, and the
author himself, have discussed the change. The prominent combination
of Hammett-like action-diction and the Chandler-like wit, sensibility
and imagery of the earlier works segued into the predominantly
psychological involvement with the woven webs of convoluted family
ties found in the later novels.
The humor softens and the occurrence of the colorful and
forceful descriptive vernacular lessens considerably as Archer becomes
less the center of the novel and more the mind of the novel it-
self--which apparently is precisely what Macdonald intended:

> While he is a man of action, his actions are largely
> directed to putting together the stories of other people's
> lives and discovering their significance.   He is less a
> doer than a questioner, a consciousness in which the
> meanings of other lives emerge.[13]

However, the emphasis on Archer's established persona as a
conduit for fuller development of the other characters in the story
is much more remarkable in the later works.
Regardless of the technique, the reader stays involved with
Archer and is drawn into the tangled family relationships which he
unravels. Peter Wolfe sums it up nicely: "The plots grip us: we
warm to the play of the mind, the nimbleness of the dialectic, and
the delicate orchestration--amid violence--of the denouement.[14]

CONCLUSION

Until a few years ago I avoided detective stories, preferring

---

[12]Ross Macdonald, **On Crime Writing** (Santa Barbara, California:
Capra Press, 1973), p. 19.

[13]Ibid., pp. 23-24.

[14]**Dreamers Who Live Their Dreams: The World of Ross Macdonald's Novels** (Bowling Green: Bowling Green University Press,
1976), p. 38.

instead the *real* whodunits. After all, how much suspense could there
be in a story told by or centered on the main character who was
going to be around not only at the finale, but in succeeding stories?
How much reader involvement could there be if the author were
not mining the story with clues? After reading the works by this
trio of writers, it is clear that so much more was possible when
the author was not flapping about red herrings, hopping in and out
of a dozen characters' heads, and/or relying on the extraordinary
mental powers of the crime solver. These writers, having presented
narrators in differing but equally effective ways to produce compelling,
suspenseful and believable stories, have established certain reader
expectations when the new novel is labelled "in the tradition of
Hammett, Chandler and Macdonald." The reader, certainly *this* reader,
wants to revel in a well-written first-person narrative that can be
anywhere on the continuum from the professionally objective Continental Op to the reflective and knightly Marlowe to the ultracaring,
saintly, scrim-like Archer.

[Continued from page 30] following a course that would clearly
reveal--*something!*--*The Stingaree Murders*, by W. Shepard Pleasants.

But only if you're a Famous Detective:

"We can read consternation in the glazed eyes, a look of vast
surprise and complete unpreparedness. Nothing was further than
death to each victim's mind!"--*The Merrivale Mystery*, by James
Corbett.

Not a crime perhaps--

"What I sold M. Archer for 10,000 francs in his own home I
could sell him for 12,000 at the cafe. 2,500 francs more because of
the collectors all around. Is that a crime?"--*The Passenger on the
U*, by Claude Aveline.

Further Gems from the Literature

William F. Deeck

Many of the following quotations come from the writings of James Corbett. For those who enjoy the truly awful mystery novel, Corbett's *Merrivale Mystery* is highly recommended, and almost equally recommended is his *Monster of Dagenham Hall* and *Vampire of the Skies*. Each of these novels has all the qualities of an "alternate classic": bad plotting, bad characterization, bad description, bad dialogue, and an uncertain ear for the language. The excerpts below hardly do them justice. Bill Pronzini has accepted my recommendation that *The Merrivale Mystery* be included in his sequel to *Gun in Cheek*, and I look forward to his dissection of it.

Department of felicitous remarks:

"Enough to poison you for it?" His tone was skeptical. "You'd never get me to swallow that."--*The Metropolitan Opera Murders*, by Helen Traubel.

Alden said, "I'll never forget the day I married Mae--she was wearing a bustle and it busted. Say, if Ruth wants her bustle pumped up, I'm just the man--"
That went uncomfortably flat.--*If a Body*, by George Worthing Yates.

"Plaza 3-7918," Emily read aloud. "Henry, doesn't that ring a bell?"--*The Corpse with One Shoe*, by Margaret Scherf.

Neatest tricks of the week:

"It is a single-chambered revolver ...."--*The Merrivale Mystery*, by James Corbett.

"The other two half-brothers are developing into congenital idiots."--*The Merrivale Mystery*, by James Corbett.

He looked up, his eyes snarling viciously ...."--*The Ebony Bed Murder*, by Rufus Gillmore.

Marjorie Gavin, the stewardess, sat strapped in one of the vacant seats....--*Obelists Fly High*, by C. Daly King.

"Thank you." The interrupting click of her instrument cut the last word in half.--*The Knife Behind You*, by James Benet.

"He has full lips, and lisps his r's a little."--*The Murder at Crome House*, by G.D.H. and Margaret Cole.

"I can rush you to Dagenham Hall ... by a circuitous route."--*The Monster of Dagenham Hall*, by James Corbett.

Nastiest trick of the week:

"Have you a cigarette?" she asked.
Cavanagh threw his case on the desk.
"You seem upset?" he suggested, lighting a match and holding it to her lips.--*Red Dagger*, by James Corbett.

Someone must have a hearty appetite:

"It's what you might call a plum, this job," went on Rolland. "Free board at the Fleur-de-Lys. Free meals at the Haute Cuisine Restaurant...."--*Death with Blue Ribbon*, by Leo Bruce.

How's-that-again? department:

"It is a mere matter of tracing backward from cause to effect, that is all."--*Murder on the Palisades*, by Will Levinrew.

Had Tabitha's words impressed Serge with real significance, and despite his protest at their incredulity had he given reality to the statement?--*The Merrivale Mystery*, by James Corbett.

Freddie's tongue shot out between his lips like the fangs of a poisonous snake.--*The Tunnel Mystery*, by J.C. Lenehan.

His brown eyes blazed at sullen intervals.--*The Merrivale Mystery*, by James Corbett.

"Dr. Sevier, the local medico, has no delusions that her end was unnatural.... He has come to the conviction that Miss Watson was murdered...."--*The Monster of Dagenham Hall*, by James Corbett.

"If ever I saw fear on a man's face, he had it written all over him...."--*The Monster of Dagenham Hall*, by James Corbett.

I felt pity for her dish rang.--*Embrace the Wolf*, by Benjamin M. Schutz.

"Was it only fancy, or did she hear the sound of a man breathing, restrained and laboured, as if hiding in there and keeping wonderfully quiet?"--*The Monster of Dagenham Hall*, by James Corbett.

The tension in Iris' chest built up unbearably. By rights, the hooks on her bra ought to snap.--*Dog Eat Dog*, by Mary Collins.

30   William F. Deeck, "Further Gems from the Literature"

"Your steps are feline and cat-like."--*The Merrivale Mystery*, by James Corbett.

From two to five in the afternoon, the dog show would really be a rat race.--*Dog Eat Dog*, by Mary Collins.

His brain was in a whirl of tumult....--*The Merrivale Mystery*, by James Corbett.

"It may be only a theoretical surmise...."--*The Monster of Dagenham Hall*, by James Corbett.

"There is no harm in putting her wise to a danger she may run from some unsuspecting source...."--*The Monster of Dagenham Hall*, by James Corbett.

"She knew Masefield would inspect that room at the first opportunity, but he never did things according to schedule, and that, she felt, might be one of them."--*The Monster of Dagenham Hall*, by James Corbett.

I was paralized to the spot!--*Three Short Biers*, by Jimmy Starr.

Almost the four corners of the U.S.A. are represented: Massachusetts, Wisconsin, Kansas, New Jersey.--*The Will and Last Testament of Constance Cobble*, by Stanton Forbes.

They knew the anticlimax was at hand, and their satisfaction was unbounded.--*The Merrivale Mystery*, by James Corbett.

Finger-print experts had spent some time in the carriage, and Maxton had loaned his microscopic aid.--*Red Dagger*, by James Corbett.

"I must enter that library unobserved, so keep your revolvers handy."--*The Merrivale Mystery*, by James Corbett.

On the other side a man in a uniform clanged the door shut behind me. Now I knew how Jimmy Cagney felt in *The Big House*.--*Death and Blintzes*, by Dorothy and Sidney Rosen.

Although they respected him as a brilliant colleague, they had an instinctive sense that he was mediocre.--*The Merrivale Mystery*, by James Corbett.

The Famous Detective pontificates:

"Mr. George Merrivale has been a hopeless invalid for years--I can see that with my own eyes...."--*The Merrivale Mystery*, by James Corbett.

Amateur detectives are easily pleased:

I could hardly wait to begin the investigation. Somehow, I firmly believed that (at last!) we were [Continued on page 27]

The Cream of Queen

Frank Floyd

NOVEMBER-DECEMBER

John Mortimer. "Rumpole and the Sporting Life."

Besides epic poetry, none of the major classes of literature is quite as difficult to write as consistently excellent short mysteries. "Consistently" is the key word. Writers of great epics in the English language are almost non-existent, and so are writers who can consistently write excellent short mysteries.

That is why I was so glad to see EQMM reprint "Rumpole and the Sporting Life." It is long enough to be less demanding on writer and reader. I would welcome an occasional story in EQMM with the high quality of this one and a length of up to fifteen thousand words or even more.

One morning at breakfast She Who Must Be Obeyed said, "We're going to the bar races on Saturday, aren't we?" The "aren't we?" really had no meaning; it just gave Rumpole the opportunity to agree. Yes, Mrs. Rumpole (we learn that She is called Hilda or Mrs. Rumpole in Her presence). On Saturday it was "tally ho" and off to the races. You see, She Who Must Be Obeyed's daddy always went to the bar races.

This story, while plainly and distinctly Mortimer's, reminds me of other writers. The horse-racing background reminds me of Dick Francis. The names of the characters remind me of Charles Dickens-- Jonathan Postern, Jeremy Jowling, and Mr. Justice Twyburne; Postern was one of the riders, Jowling was a solicitor. The Yorkshire quaintness in a character or two reminds me of James Herriot.

There is in Mortimer's tale some wry homely humor. There is a clue so well placed that it is embarrassing when it is revealed. I was saved from feeling humiliated by having guessed the solution without it. Rumpole is in court as the defendant's barrister and out of court as the discoverer of clues. Rumpole in court does not remind me of Perry Mason. His style is different, being less single-minded. She Who Must Be Obeyed reminds me of Rudyard Kipling.

JANUARY-FEBRUARY

Robert Henson. "Lizzie Borden in the P.M."

EQMM is an untiring rescuer of dust-laden crime and mystery
stories from fading pages and oblivion. Compared to most, this one
is relatively new. First published in *The Quarterly Review of Literature*, it was an O. Henry Award winner, finishing second in 1974.

It is about Lizzie Borden in later life, until death, as told by
her sister, Emma Borden, although each detail and thought always
reflects back to Lizzie Borden's guilt or innocence. Without ever
once saying so directly, Henson attempts in the story to show what
kind of person Lizzie Borden was and whether it was possible for
her to have hacked her father and step-mother to death with an
ax. There is plenty to think on.

A dramatic picture of the Bordens' lives begins gradually to
appear. The Borden family was fairly well off for the time. The
girls' real mother had died, and their father pampered them, especially
Lizzie, who sometimes made self-centered and unreasonable demands.
After several years, their father remarried. The girls were jealous
of the new Mrs. Borden, and their father failed in his continuous
efforts to maintain a degree of harmony among the three of them.
Before long, Mrs. Borden began spending much of her day alone in
her room upstairs, often emerging only to eat. She became a glutton
and, from Lizzie and Emma's point of view, antisocial. Shortly
before the murders, a little gold watch and some jewelry were
stolen from Mrs. Borden's dressing table. A quiet suspicion within
the family fell on Lizzie. Mr. Borden asked that the police discon-
tinue their investigation. Afterwards, the door between Lizzie's
room and the room in which her father and step-mother slept,
which had not been locked before, was always kept locked. Lizzie
would admit nothing. She never would own up to being wrong at
any time. She responded to the locked door by fixing a lock on
her side of the door, too.

The rest of the story ... is in your January EQMM.

Regardless of your feelings about an author putting words into
the mouths of people who lived and didn't say them, you will have
to affirm, upon reading "Lizzie Borden in the P.M.," that Robert
Henson has done a fine and perceptive piece of writing, one costing
him boundless labors.

It's About Crime

Marvin Lachman

Richard Stevenson's *Death Trick* (St. Martin's Press, 1981, $10.95) is an affirmative action mystery. In this first book in a series about Don Strachey, Albany, New York, private detective, Stevenson makes homosexuals the "good guys" while every single non-homosexual character is portrayed as stupid, bigoted, or venal. Granting that Hammett, Chandler, and many other mystery writers provided unfavorable portraits of homosexuals, it does not seem to be to be progress to do likewise with the entire "straight" community.

Perhaps "True Confessions" might have been a more appropriate title for this book, since much of it involves male homosexuals describing how they first became aware of their sexual orientation. There is also considerable space devoted to almost non-stop promiscuity, a blur of young men flitting from one bed to another. Though Stevenson has admitted that he (like Strachey) is homosexual, it seems strange that he would deliberately portray that alternate life style in terms which are so unflattering. Incidentally, when the characters are not in bed they are dancing to disco music at homosexual bars, and the book's 190 pages contain continuous references to groups and songs of which I have never heard.

As a detective story *Death Trick* isn't bad, though the plot is very simple. An establishment couple hires Strachey to locate their son, a homosexual who is suspected of a murder. Strachey does not do anything that qualifies him as any great sleuth, and the mystery is resolved without much mental exertion on his part. In fact, had Strachey told the police what he suspected, a murder could have been avoided. But then Stevenson's hero would be violating the long tradition of private detectives in withholding information from the police. Still, the setting (Albany) is unusual, the narration is crisp, and Strachey at times makes a witty, intelligent protagonist. While Stevenson tries to make him Likable, I soon grew tired of his venomous descriptions of his clients. The book's nadir is reached when Strachey deliberately rips them off for $2,000, which he contributes to a homosexual defense fund.

I'm pleased that Harcourt, Brace, Jovanovich has decided to reprint William De Andrea's Edgar-winning 1978 first novel, *Killed in the Ratings* (Harvest paperback, $4.95), since it was one of the best debuts of recent years. It was also the debut of Matt Cobb, troubleshooter at the New York headquarters of a large television network. He is called in when it appears that someone has been rigging the ratings by which television programs' popularity are measured. Then, murder strikes among the executive staff of the network, and Cobb finds more than a job involved; he has to prove himself innocent of the killings. He's a refreshing hero, willing to admit when he's scared, as he should be, caught between police and killer. Typical of the author's light touch is Cobb's joke that he is so chicken that he was drafted in the first round by Frank Perdue. In the book's very first sentence De Andrea has Cobb describe the network headquarters as the "Tower of Babble." De Andrea never fails to poke fun at television whenever he can, but there is also a certain affection and nostalgia on his part, e.g. his chapter openings, which are famous lines from early television shows and commercials.

De Andrea knows his New York, and he uses the city beautifully, beginning with his reference to Sixth Avenue: "Only the tourists and letterheads say 'Avenue of the Americas.'" As Cobb races around the city, usually one step ahead of police and gangsters, we get many excellent descriptions of various aspects of city life, including the subways and Times Square. Cobb, for all his self-depreciation, proves to be an effective and resourceful detective. After this book Bill De Andrea went on to win another Edgar and to become one of the most prolific and varied mystery writers around. It's hard to believe it is less than a decade since this book appeared, but that was long enough to make it unavailable, except from used book dealers. Readers who have not read it can be thankful to HBJ for making it available again.

Although I had read P.D. James before, I had only read her two Cordelia Gray books and her non-series novel *Innocent Blood*. I thought it was high time I started the Adam Dalgleish series which brought her fame. If *Cover Her Face* (1962), her first book, reprinted by Warner and available for $3.50, is any example, her reputation is well-deserved. She shows what happens when someone who can write really well tackles all the traditional elements of the classic mystery, in this case murder during a weekend at an Essex estate hosting the local village's annual summer fete. We get a well-clued detective story, but one in which all of the characters come alive and so we care who killed whom on an intellectual *and* an emotional level. We also enjoy identifying with Dalgleish, "the cultured cop," as one character dubs him because he is sophisticated but also a person who has gone through tragedy in his own life and never treats murder as if it is trivial.

"Classic" is a word tossed around lightly these days, but R. Austin Freeman's *The Red Thumb Mark* (1907; reprinted by Dover Books in trade paperback at $5.95) is one book which deserves that term. It's Freeman's first book in the Dr. Thorndyke series, which lasted about forty years. It includes the memorable meeting (actually a reunion) between Thorndyke and his "Watson" and fellow doctor, Jervis. Freeman is known for later popularizing the "inverted" mystery, in which the reader knows the criminal but is kept in suspense as to how the detective will solve the case.

The Red Thumb Mark, however, is a classic detective story, though there are not many suspects, and you probably will have little trouble guessing the culprit. What makes it so readable after almost eighty years is the great story-telling gift of the author, even if he sometimes included some purple prose, as in this example of Jervis, unhappy in love, saying, "But no sorrow that I had hitherto experienced could compare with the grief that I now felt in contemplating the irretrievable ruin of what I knew to be the great passion of my life." An entire book of that would be unbearable, but the doses are small enough so they only make for nice touches of nostalgia. On the other hand, we get Freeman's lecture on fingerprints, the equivalent of Carr on Locked Rooms. There are also some nice touches of humor, including the dotty woman who gives hilarious testimony on the witness stand during the book's climactic trial. It follows an especially good bit of writing as Freeman describes the swearing-in of the jury as "half-solemn and half grotesque, with an effect intermediate between that of a religious rite and a comic opera."

I'll gladly go through the entire alphabet with Sue Grafton's Kinsey Millhone because she writes *good* private eye novels. However, despite her early promise, it begins to appear that Grafton will never write a *great* mystery. *"C" Is for Corpse* (Scribner's, $14.95) is not a step forward in her career, perhaps even a pace or two backwards. She starts off by giving away the name of the victim on page *one*, and that is a bad mistake since he is an unusually interesting character and doesn't get killed until almost page *one hundred*. For what purpose did Grafton undermine her own suspense: the dubious effect of a dramatic opening line?

In this book Grafton has cut back a bit on her overuse of similes, but she still overwrites, giving unnecessary detail. We do not need to know each time Kinsey showers after jogging. These details do not make for character development. I wish Grafton would spend the extra time in making Millhone a character who relies more on her brains and less on pure guts and luck to solve her cases. As late as page 223 Kinsey is moaning, "I don't know what it means.... This case is just starting to break and I just can't figure out what's going on." Well, when you're the author and *you* can't figure it out, you send your heroine wandering around a deserted hospital morgue, without her gun, and with the murderer tracking her. After all, that kind of ending worked in *"B" as in Burglar*, which won several awards. It makes for an exciting conclusion, even if it doesn't make Millhone an intelligent private eye. Don't be put off by all the negatives I've cited. If you like private eye stories, you'll enjoy Grafton very much. It's just that I am disappointed when I see potential unrealized.

In the last three years or so Carroll and Graf has joined Dover and Perennial Library in the ranks of the most imaginative publishers with their reprints of older, otherwise unavailable works. In the past they reprinted the Inspector Hanaud mysteries of A.E.W. Mason, and out-of-print works by Thomas B. Dewey and Anthony Boucher, among others. Now they are sampling Freeman Wills Crofts' works, including *Inspector French's Greatest Case* (1925). This classic detective story, despite its immodest title which is uncharacteristic of the unassuming Crofts, launched a series character whose specialty was breaking the seemingly unbreakable alibi. This story of murder at a London jeweler's does not depend as much on alibis as later work, but, nonetheless, it is a complicated mystery, brought to a logical, satisfying solution. Again, as with R. Austin Freeman (are we confused on the names?), the old-fashioned qualities are a bonus, though the story telling is crisp, clean, and reasonably modern sounding.

John Dickson Carr has been dead more than a decade, but if the extent to which he is reprinted and the interest which attended a talk about him at the last Bouchercon is any indication, he is still "alive." Carroll and Graf have published many Carr books in the past and now have reprinted representative titles for two of his series sleuths. *In Spite of Thunder* (1960) is one of the last entries in the Gideon Fell series, and if not up to the author's

early work from the 1930s, it is still very worthwhile. In addition
to his impossible crimes, in this book Carr creates an atmosphere
of a thunderstorm about to break which raises the hackles from the
reader's neck.

The Lost Gallows (1931) was a book about Carr's first series
detective, Henri Bencolin, the French detective who is in London
investigating a bizarre crime involving traditional British Punch and
Judy shows. Here, Carr does a masterful job of using London's fog
to give the reader a sense of mood, with a feeling of dampness
which permeates the bones.

Cornell Woolrich has been dead even longer than Carr (1968),
but his popularity seems to be growing. Carroll and Graf has reached
into the crumbling pulp magazines of the late 1930s for the four
stories in Vampire's Honeymoon. I don't like horror fiction especially, but leave it to Woolrich to do a story about vampires that is so
convincing with its own inner reality that I almost ended up believing
in them. The other three stories are equally suspenseful, if also
unlikely. "Graves for the Living" is about being buried alive, a
frequent fear of Woolrich. "I'm Dangerous Tonight" is one of the
books in that small sub-genre Woolrich created, mysteries in which
dresses (!) are weapons. "Street of Jungle Death" was cannibalized
to become the novel Black Alibi, but it stands very nicely on its
own as an exciting tale of a leopard loose in Hollywood.

All of the above Carroll and Graf books sell for $3.50. Carroll
and Graf's slimmer volume, Edgar Wallace's Four Just Men, sells for
only $2.95. This thriller can only be recommended for nostalgia
and history. It involves terrorism and murder, supposedly in a
worthy political cause, but the plot is not especially believable, and
too much blood has been spilled by terrorists since the book first
appeared in 1905 for one not to have reservations about it. Still,
Wallace was one of the most prolific and popular mystery writers
this side of John Creasey, and this book was a major success. It's
a fast read and just might appeal to readers who want to know
what caused Wallace to be so successful in his time as a mystery
writer. Some people only remember him now as one of the screen
writers of King Kong.

Reel Murders
(Movie Reviews)

Walter Albert

BLUE VELVET

I have never listened to much popular music--other than show music--and for all I know Bobby Vinton's recording of "Blue Velvet" may be a period piece that captures the feeling of a year or even of a decade. Whatever its importance as a popular icon, David Lynch has used it effectively in his film *Blue Velvet* where the plushy, languorous singing, returning insistently like a haunting refrain, provides an erotic, languorous counterpoint to the often brutal events of a film that, like Lynch's first movie, *Eraserhead*, shows some promise of becoming a cult classic.

Kyle Maclachlan, the apple-cheeked hero of Lynch's film of Frank Herbert's science-fiction epic novel, *Dune*, plays a seemingly innocent hero who, like the heroine of many an insufferable Gothic romance, blunders against all good sense into a situation in which his life and even his virtue are at peril. Lunch's intention is, in part, satiric--as it was in the memorable *Eraserhead*--and, against the background of an idealized all-American city captured in colors that have the intensity of pop art painting, Kyle/Jeffrey, obsessed with the masochistic needs of a sexually tormented singer--played by Isabella Rossellini--attempts to unravel the intricate psycho-sexual empire presided over by a demented Dennis Hopper.

Maclachlan is aided by a somewhat mature Nancy Drew, splendidly portrayed by blond Laura Dern, the "good" woman in his life (as sultry, raven-haired Rossellini is his "dark" mistress), who, in some perplexity, asks him if he is a "pervert" or a detective. Summoning up as much of a leer as his somewhat limited acting skill will allow, Maclachlan replies that it is for "me to know and you to find out." This gauntlet is, of course, also thrown down to the sometimes bemused viewer and this Chinese-box film, with its blue velvet song and fabric serving as an opening and closing frame, will not find a disinterested audience. If some equivalent of the League for Moral Decency is still functioning, an extended sequence in which Rossellini seduces a fascinated but somewhat reluctant hero into a sado-masochistic tumble should have its adherents taking to the streets in self-righteous outrage. Maclachlan keeps protesting that he only wants to help while Rossellini pleads with him to hurt her and it is this psychological ambivalence that lies at the heart (and it is an amused and perverse intelligence which controls it) of this brilliantly directed film.

Blue Velvet is impeccably cast and often memorably played. Rossellini and Hopper are an unforgettable apparently mismatched

pair, while former MGM child star Dean Stockwell plays the stoned
proprietor of a peculiarly staffed whorehouse with deadly, pointillist
accuracy.   Once again, Lynch has shown a particular genius for
undermining the American family.   Machlachlan's father, mother,
and aunt are Grant Wood figures in a Charles Burchfield darkling
wood. Not to be missed are the quick shots of the family's prime-
time TV viewing and the robin-with-beetle episode that closes the
film. Whatever your view of small-town America may be, it is not
likely to be the same after seeing this absorbing movie.   Do not
expect to be moved or to care about the characters' fates.   Some
viewers will feel the film is an assault on basic virtues and common
decency, and it is. Others will revel in the photography, delight in
the often witty script, and find in themselves unsuspected depths
of playful decadence in their response to *Blue Velvet*. The viewer
is invited to become a detective but also to participate vicariously
in the complex games Lynch plays. And it is up to you, dear reader,
should you see this film, to answer that provocative question posed
by Laura/"Nancy" to Kyle/Jeffrey. But you may not want to share
your answer with your best friend, your lover ... or yourself.

SHORT TAKE

Freaks. Tod Browning's 1932 circus melodrama classic has been
issued on videocassette in an immaculate print.   Some audiences
have found the film disturbing in its use of circus freaks as per-
formers, but it is not the people with the physical abnormalities
who are the true freaks in this moving drama.   Browning was a
master of melodramatic horror and directed several of Lon Chaney's
finest performances. The compassion the spectator felt for Chaney's
portrayals was not entirely due to that great actor's gifts, and two
sequences in this short film are memorable: the freaks surprised
while out on a picnic in the country, and the wedding feast that
has some of the richness of a Bosch painting.   The print at my
local video outlet has been supplied with a crude "warning" that
this is a black-and-white film.   Indeed it is and often of great
beauty. The film also includes a short epilogue which I had not
seen before. Highly recommended.

Verdicts
(Book Reviews)

Guy M. Townsend. *To Prove a Villain.* Perseverance Press, 1985, 190 pp., $6.95. *[What's the point of being editor if you can't give yourself top billing, huh?]*

Marian James-Tyrell, head of the English Department at Brookleigh College, good-looking, intelligent, rich, available for an extramarital fling with the right person, is smothered to death with a pillow at home in bed. John Forest becomes involved in the investigation of her death because he is curious about the murder of a fellow faculty member, because Lieutenant Ben Latta in charge of the investigation is a student in one of his night classes and the reporter doing the story of the local paper is a woman with whom he once had a non-marital fling, and because there seems to be a relationship between Marian James-Tyrell's death and the murder of thirteen-year-old Edward V and his younger brother in 1483 by order by order of their uncle, Richard III, which is, Forest being a history professor, right up his alley.

If for no other reason, *To Prove a Villain* is a pleasure to read on account of its good prose, dispelling the generally held silly notion that good grammar and mystery cannot cohabit the same pages. Everyone will detect the absence of dehumanized gore and aggrandized sex; by this absence the book is made more realistic, contrary to what the carping and prattling in print for the last thirty years would lead us all to expect.

John Forest's letter from his father is one of the most effective letters in fiction. It is so believable that I am certain it must have had as its basis a letter written in real life to the author.

To my notion the main accomplishment of the book was touched on by Marvin Lachman in his "It's About Crime" column in *The Mystery Fancier* (November/December 1986): "A considerable amount of the book is devoted to the relationship of the narrator and his deceased father. While this could be regarded as extraneous, I found it made sleuth John Miles Forest more of a real person. Townsend's writing about father-son relations was more perceptive and moving than many a 'mainstream' novel on the same subject."

In fact, Townsend has discovered the long-sought route-to-the-Orient of mystery writing--the way to write a "mainstream" mystery novel. He has combined the many-threaded story and personal interest approach of novels of years gone by--*A Tale of Two Cities, Barnaby Rudge, Silas Marner*--with a modern type mystery story and first person narration. The blueprint is there for others to follow and write by.

The parts of *To Prove a Villain* add up to more than the
whole, however. Townsend made several little slips of his pen in
integrating and rounding out his story. His most consistent fault
throughout the book is telling us what happened instead of letting
us see it happen. I closed the novel feeling as though John Forest
had been giving a long dramatic monologue or a soliloquy. I hardly
"saw" the other characters move about and do anything.

I read the book two times and enjoyed it more the second
time. I trust the same will be true of the third. (Frank Floyd)

Nicholas Blake. *Malice in Wonderland.* Harper, 1940 (Penguin, 1946).

In the thirties and forties C. Day Lewis was one of England's
leading younger poets. He was also writing mysteries and publishing
them under the pen name of Nicholas Blake. I do not know how
his reputation as a poet has fared, but his mysteries continue to be
reprinted, read, and reread. They are literate and cunningly plotted,
as well as psychologically astute. If his amateur detective, Nigel
Strangeways, at times appears distressingly juvenile, he is usually
likable and considerably less omniscient than many of his breed.

The site of *Malice in Wonderland* is a British summer holiday
camp, analogous in some ways to the more organized summer resorts
in this country. I found when reading Paul Theroux's *Kingdom by
the Sea* that the thirties Wonderland has its contemporary counterpart
in Butlin's Holiday Camps, which Theroux found depressing. Wonderland is a summer camp for grownups, as organized with games and
activities as such camps generally are for children and youths. To
this Wonderland comes young Paul Perry, a "mass observer." He
plans to take copious notes on his experience to impress his boss
and win a full-time job. On the way he meets the Thistlethwaite
family, Mr., Mrs., and attractive daughter, Sally. Mr. T. is a master
tailor in Oxford, and very conscious of his high status compared to
most of Wonderland's visitors. The camp is indeed a wonderland
for its lower middle-class residents, who come to get the most for
their money on their brief vacations. There is a modernistic main
building for dining and indoor activities; there are comfortable
chalets to live in; there is sea bathing, a fun fair, and even a Pet
Corner so that pets don't have to be left at home.

Unfortunately, there is trouble in Wonderland. A ragged
hermit lives in the nearby woods; he bears a grudge against the
camp for taking his previous living space, and so from time to time
he jumps out, naked, and frightens the visitors. In the camp itself
there is a practical joker whose jokes get progressively rougher.
He, or she, takes on the title of the Mad Hatter.

As the paying guests get more nervous, the camp staff decide
to take action. Director Mortimer Wise, his secretary, Esmeralda
Jones, and his brother, activities director Teddy Wise, enlist Paul's
help in devising a questionnaire that might give them some pointers
to the joker. But the "jokes" only escalate. Dead animals from
the woods are found in people's beds; a little dog in the Pet Corner
is poisoned; a young woman's arm breaks out in huge blisters after
a treasure hunt. The word somehow leaks out and reservations are
cancelled. Faced with what could be the end of Wonderland, the
staff go along with Mr. T.'s suggestion that they call in Nigel
Strangeways, one of his former Oxford gentlemen who has had
considerable experience in detection.

Paul, Sally, Teddy, Esmeralda, and Mortimer circle one another, moving to and fro in a metaphorical mating dance. Albert Morley, a born butt of practical jokes, makes one wonder if he can possibly go through life as a worm that never turns. Old Ishmael turns out to be more of a mystery than he at first appears. Nigel considers them all as suspects. He sorts out the occurrences, and with the help of the questionnaire, puts the red herrings to one side and finds a consistent pattern to the rest. In one final Mad Hatter's tea party, he exposes the plot.

Blake is lavish in his description of the attractions of a working-class holiday paradise. Meals served, no housework to do, lots of games and entertainment from talent shows to shooting gallery, and the opportunity to meet others of the opposite sex, if you are young and single. Yet he shows us few real working-class people. Miss Jones has fallen from a higher station; Mortimer Wise was a captain in the armed forces; Perry is a white–collar worker; Thistle-thwaite is quite conscious of being a superior sort of tradesman. A few peripheral characters, drawn lightly, are the only working–class people around. Blake found it easier to write of the kinds of people he knew, and in doing so no doubt he was wise. The camp itself is a great scene for mysterious goings-on, and Mr. T., in particular, is a wondrous creation.

There is plenty of mystery and plenty of detection, though nary a murder. (Maryell Cleary)

Sister Carol Anne O'Marie.   *Advent of Dying*.   Delacorte Press, 1986, 227 pp., $14.95.

Sister Carol Anne O'Marie writes a creditable mystery story. In *Advent of Dying* she picks up from her first novel, *Novena for Murder* (1984), which introduced Sister Mary Helen, a seventy–five–year–old nun who is an ardent mystery–novel reader and a recent sleuth.

The world of Sister Mary Helen is a college owned by her religious order. She has been persuaded to return there after retirement to an administrative job at the fictitious Mount St. Francis College for Women. In this second novel, the personalities of Sister Mary Helen's friends are now clearly defined. Sister Eileen, her faithful friend of fifty years with whom she was in the novitiate, is the most enjoyable, with her bright sense of humor and attempts to protect Mary Helen. Sister Anne presents the innovative younger attitudes with her devotion to yoga and her choice of jeans and Berkenstock sandals. Mary Helen is fond of Anne although often amused by her. Mary Helen said she was "positive God was male, no matter what Sister Anne said."

There is a good deal of good-natured, non–scholarly religion in the story, as there was in the first book. With the exception of that in the subplot, the religious flavor is all perfectly pleasant and easily worked in. The subplot, however, attempts to present the lay perspective in the lives of the young couple Detective Kate Murphy and her husband Jack Bassetti. In *Novena*, Kate finally agrees to marry her live-in mate, Jack, after long nagging by Jack and his mother (and encouragement by Mary Helen). In *Advent*, Kate finally agrees to try to get pregnant after long-suffering suggestions by Jack, more nagging by Mama Bassetti, and broad hints by the protagonist nun. Kate and Jack have recently returned to going to

weekly Mass with only nagging of conscience. The device of including
a lay couple to provide details outside the convent or rectory is
also used by William Kienzle in his Father Koesler series. Kienzle
handles it a little more smoothly and less sentimentally, however.

The organization of the plot around the days of Advent preceding
Christmas contains the suspense very nicely. It is more effective
than the nine divisions (nine days) of the novena in the first novel
because of the possibility of more small chunks of time and the
wider appeal of the anticipation of Christmas morning.

O'Marie puts more into the structure of the story than into
the establishment of characters this time. She builds suspense by
having Sister Mary Helen move steadily and dangerously closer to
the solution in spite of the serious efforts of Detective Murphy and
the semi-serious ones of Sister Eileen to keep her safely out of it.
Mary Helen listens, reasons, and acts according to the models of
the detectives in the mysteries she reads as well as according to
the customs of her social and moral conscience. Mary Helen is less
overbearing here than in the first book, and her reasoning is less
obvious.

It will be a pleasure to read the next O'Marie and to anticipate
the next church-event title that will accommodate a numbered
sequence of activities. (Martha Alderson)

Donald E. Westlake. *Good Behavior.* Mysterious Press, 1986, 244
pp., $15.95.

No need to open the envelope; Donald E. Westlake wins the
award for most schizophrenic mystery writer in a walk. As no one
needs to be told who's read his twenty crime novels under the
pseudonym of Richard Stark, when he is grim he is very very grim.
But when he puts on his clown suit, as he usually does when publishing under his own byline, he's the funniest thriller writer alive.
In his novels about comic badman John Dortmunder, we watch that
mad genius assemble a pickup team of inept thieves for a multi-
million-dollar caper, and then we see the same kinds of glitches
crawl out of the woodwork as we do in the Richard Stark novels
when the ruthless heist man Parker assembles *his* team of amoral
professionals for a Big Caper of their own. But in the Dortmunders
all the twists of fate and fortune are played out in a lighthearted
other-side-of-the-rabbit-hole world where no one is allowed to be
killed or raped or tortured or even to be bruised badly. It's the
world of the fairy tale, probably the closest thing to the world of
P.G. Wodehouse that any American has conjured up. And it's pure
joy to spend a few hours there.

Dortmunder and his gang-that-couldn't-steal-straight are back
for their sixth caper in *Good Behavior*, and a fine mess it is.
Escaping from the New York police across a block of rooftops,
Dortmunder literally falls through the roof of the convent of the
Silent Sisters of St. Filumena, an order of nuns whose vows forbid
them to speak except for two hours every Thursday. With the help
of charades they explain to Dortmunder that God himself has hurled
him into their lives. Their youngest and newest member, Sister
Mary Grace, is being held in a luxury apartment on the seventy-
sixth floor of a Manhattan bank tower by her evil father and his
deprogrammers. This father is so wealthy and so powerful that it's
useless even to think about going to the police or a lawyer or

Geraldo Rivera; no, only a burglar who is also a mad genius can possibly rescue the maiden from the tower. Dortmunder signs on, recruits as his accomplices the usual gang of idiots (a Frankenstein's Monster type, a woman who sells Scandinavian Marriage Secrets books, a senile ex-jailbird drooling with propositions for every female he encounters), and prepares for his assault on the castle-- and on several wholesale jewelers' shops that happen to be located in the bank building. Before the caper is over, the new Saint John is mistaken for a mercenary soldier of fortune, shanghaied into a private war in South America,k chased up and down seventy-six floors of fire stairs by storm troopers, shoved unceremoniously into a dishwasher--you name it, Dortmunder suffers it.

Of course, as in Wodehouse, this is all a delicate tracery of nonsense, plotted with a corkscrew, written with touches of magic, wildly unlikely if looked at with a cold keen eye, but credible and even inevitable within the lunatic logic of the Westlake world. A few moments in the book's final chapter don't mesh well with the gossamer fabric, but all in all this is one of the most pleasurable novels in years. Whoever misses Westlake misses American crime fiction at its funniest. (Francis M. Nevins, Jr.)

Rick Boyer. *The Daisy Ducks.* Houghton, Mifflin, 1986, 276 pp., $15.95.

In Doc Adams' third outing, he's involved with his martial arts instructor and the instructor's old 'Nam buddies in a seek-and-destroy mission that takes Adams from Concord, Massachusetts (his home town), into the wilds of North Carolina.

Doc has the itch for adventure again, but this time it's Rambo instead of Sherlock Holmes. In the past, Boyer has kept Doc in New England and Boyer's knowledge of the area showed in the great local color. Now that Boyer has become a resident of North Carolina, how hard it is to find the reason for Doc's temporary (I hope!) relocation.

The book is uneven in its pacing. The first half develops slowly, and then it's hell for leather to the end. When Boyer is "on," as in the second half of *The Daisy Ducks,* he's right on. This book took a long time coming to press, but all in all it was worth the wait.

I still think the first book in the series (*Billingsgate Shoal*) is the best, but Boyer's potential for a great mystery-suspense novel will keep me coming back to find out if he has written the ultimate adventure yarn. (Alan S. Mosier)

Noel Behn. *Seven Silent Men.* Pocket Books, 1985, 472 pp.

Many readers will be aware of a double prejudice of mine, freely and frequently admitted. I make no excuse for part of it. It works for me, and I recommend it to others: let the fat books sink to the bottom of the to-be-read stack (if you are going to keep them at all). There are, of course, exceptions. Spy books are also sinkers for me. Yes, I like them, and read many, but I like them *less* than several other mystery subgenres, so they have to wait for my attention. Just a matter of taste.

On rare occasions I plumb the depths. Recently, remembering

how much I enjoyed *The Kremlin Letter* and *The Shadowboxer*
(both still highly recommended!), I raised this book for a read. Oh,
happy decision!

Mix in equal parts: a caper novel that would do credit to
Westlake, the best sinister secret organization this side of *The Man
Who Was Thursday*, and a cop novel that Joe Wambaugh could be
proud of (except that these "cops" are FBI agents), and you have
the recipe. However, with such disparate parts, few writers but
Behn could bring off the combination.

Seven Silent Men begins with the caper, the robbery of a
suburban bank on the eve of its opening. Of course, as they always
seem to, a few things go wrong. The local FBI, soon augmented by
biggies from Washington, including old J. Edgar himself (the story
is set in 1971 in a mythical Missouri metropolis, Prairie Point, that
has outgrown St. Louis), investigate. The biggies' announced reason
for their participation is that a huge and secret transfer of federal
funds was in the vault, just long enough to become part of the
loot. In the course of the Bureau's investigation a local agent is
murdered. Ah ha! The master criminals must have felt the master
investigators were getting too close!

The investigation, mostly in the hands of a misfit hero, proceeds
and keeps turning up bits and pieces that make little or no sense.
Each time the biggies come back, often (the hero thinks) more to
discredit the new evidence than to look into what it may mean.
Suspicious, naturally enough, he begins to investigate the FBI--and
becomes a target for assassination.

Still pressing on, even after becoming a wanted man himself,
he unearths a sinister plot too fantastic to summarize. The Director
himself even seems involved. While in the final solution, after
much derring-do that also defies summarization, J. Edgar turns out
(like a multitude of others) to have been merely a dupe, the plotters
are fully unmasked, and the original robbery solved.

I believe this is Behn's best book, and considering my especial
fondness for *The Kremlin Letter* that is high praise indeed. Find
it. Read it. Enjoy, enjoy! (Jeff Banks)

The Documents in the Case
(Letters)

From William F. Deeck, 9020 Autoville Drive, College Park, MD
20740:

Fred Isaac's "Looking Glass Detection: The Norths and Bill
Weigand Speak" gave me some fresh insight into the—I started to
say Mr. and Mrs. North novels, but I guess it should be novel that
have Mr. and Mrs. North in them. Something had bothered me
about them, and now I know what it was. Heimrich, however,
appeared in at least two of the novels with Mr. and Mrs. North.
At least Heimrich says, in *Death of a Tall Man*, that he remembered
them from another case, which sounded like the North's first.
(This is not excellent memory on my part, I hasten to add; I just
got through reading *Death of a Tall Man*.)

Strange. I wrote to Garland a few months back asking for a
catalogue since I had heard something about the college–mystery–
novel bibliography. The material they sent me did not include that
or some of the other reference works you mention. But then publishers have always been peculiar creatures. Selling books seems to
be beneath them. I guess they fear people will think they're in
the business for money.

[A later letter:]

The back issues of TMF arrived safely and were devoured
almost immediately. Your subscribers who don't have those older
volumes are missing out on some fascinating material. Well, except
for the stuff about Eddie Drood, who has never stirred me particular-
ly.

The old feuds also grabbed me. I'm glad that the quotation-
and–punctuation question was resolved, after its fashion, before I
became a subscriber. I have made up my mind which way I will do
it and I think I've decided which is the right way, which, of course,
is not the way I do it.

Engrossing also was where you were likely to be sojourning
each issue. I have heard of peripatetic philosophers, but a peripatetic
editor is new to me.

I was also very pleased with Volume 1 of *The Armchair Detective*.
A fine job. I really thought I was an original subscriber, but discovered recently that my first issue was Volume 2, No. 4. Why I
never subscribed early on to TMF is likely to be an enduring mystery
since I, who ought to know, have no explanation.

Reading the back issues kept me from some of my most important
activities: spending half the day deciding which book from my
collection I should read or reread and a quarter of the day sitting

in front of my VDT watching the cursor blink on an empty screen.
It seems everyone else wants to write; I want to have written.

Your Nero Wolfe saga was great stuff, even though I missed a
few episodes. I once planned something vaguely along those lines.
Since you are a Wodehouse fan, you probably are aware of Geoffrey
Jaggard's *Wooster's World* and *Blandings the Blest.* I had a notion
to try to do much the same thing for Nero Wolfe's World. Unfortunately, after buying a word processor to get started on it, I
discovered how much work it would be and how much reading I
wouldn't get done and I'd have probably screwed it up anyhow.

Since I did miss a few episodes in your saga, did you by any
chance deal with a question that has bothered me for some years
and that I do not remember having seen answered by McAleer,
Darby, or Baring-Gould? This is Archie's remark in *Fer-de-Lance*
that his parents died when he was a kid. Yet later on his mother
is still alive, and I seem to recall in one book that his father was
mentioned as also living. Has there been an explanation?

*[The "Nero Wolfe Saga" to which Bill refers was a nineteen-
part serial article which ran--all 115,000 words of it--in these
pages between 1977 and 1980. It was, believe it or not, intended
to be a mere survey of the literature, after which I intended to go
back and give the stories that comprise the saga the really complete
treatment that they deserve. As a matter of fact, I made a start
on this comprehensive research in 1981, going through the first
four novels and ferreting out every reference to everything and
everybody and compiling thousands of notes in the process. This
was in my pre-computer days, and the work involved was staggering,
but I would have kept at it had I not gotten sidetracked by something
or another. That's probably for the best, since the revolution that
has taken place in computers over past half dozen years has been
astonishing, and I've got my eye on an expensive piece of software
which seems perfectly tailored for this sort of research. I hope to
get back to it in the next year or two--unless, of course, somebody
beats me to it. I don't think that's likely to happen, though, since
doing the job right will take thousands of hours, and I don't know
anybody except myself who is crazy enough to spend so much time
on a project which will have so limited a financial return.*

*[To get to your question, Bill, I haven't read any of the saga
for six years (though just talking about it has got me to salivating),
and my recollection is too hazy to be of any use. The best I can
do is refer the question to Art Scott, who knows more about the
Saga than I ever did--possibly more than anyone but the late Jud
Sapp--and I'll be quite surprised if he can't come up with an answer
for you, complete down to chapter and verse.]*

From Bob Adey, 1 Spring Close, Colwall, Nr. Malvern, Worcestershire,
WR13 6RE, England:

Just to confirm that I am renewing my TMF sub....
This also gives me the chance to say how nice it is to see
TMF back. Other magazines have "taken a rest" with the promise
that they would return, but you're the only one that did--and the
only one I ever thought would. I don't know how you manage to
contain all your activities--but I'm very glad that you do!

Christmas has brought the usual rash of mystery oriented
goodies. A radio version of Hercule Poirot's Christmas, promise of

a televised Colin Dexter series in the New Year and original stories about Charles Paris (by Simon Brett) and Dangerous Davies (by Leslie Thomas) in the Christmas issue of the *Sunday Express*, and one about Rumpole (by John Mortimer) in the *Observer*. Oh yes, and a new Miss Marple (again with Joan Hickson)—"Murder at the Vicarage." I fear that this may be the last, as between them TV and film seem now to have used up all the Miss Marple novels—though of course there's always the 13 Problems.

From Charles Shibuk, 2084 Bronx Park East, Bronx, NY   10462:

There are a few errors in Jeff Banks' article "Spade Trumps Unplayed."
1) The Mexican Spitfire series was produced by RKO—not Warner Brothers.
2) Alison Skipworth—not Zasu Pitts—played the Caspar Gutman role in *Satan Met a Lady*.
3) The character played by Elisha Cook, Jr., in the 1941 version of *The Maltese Falcon* is named Wilmer (as in the novel)—not Wilbur.
4) The hour-long Sam Spade radio script is called *The Kandy* (not Buddah's) *Tooth Caper*.
William F. Deeck might be interested to learn that Marvin Lachman pioneered the "Further Gems from the Literature" type of column in *The Mystery Lovers' Newsletter* several years before the publication of Barzun and Taylor's *Catalogue of Crime* in 1971.

From Walker Martin, 432 Latona Ave., Trenton, NJ   08618:

I'd like to say that I'm glad you are back because I missed your magazine. I especially missed Bob Sampson's articles on the mystery and detective series that appeared in the pulps. His latest article on McBride and Kennedy in *Black Mask* was really a fine piece of work. He does original research and doesn't just repeat the same old tired comments on the popular, best selling mystery authors. I hope you can continue to encourage Bob to submit articles. The pulps were full of interesting detective series.
[I wholeheartedly endorse your words of praise, which I hope will cause Bob to shake loose another of his incomparable pieces. I think that one of TMF's main claims to fame is that it is where many of Bob's pieces first appeared in print.]

From Perry Dillon, 2009 N.W. 20th, Oklahoma City, OK   73106:

Welcome back! These last issues have been great; so, as usual, it is a pleasure to renew my subscription.
Censorship is an insidious menace, more and more threatening this country. As you know, the situation in some schools is frightening. Here in Oklahoma, cable channels are being censored, taken to court for "immorality."
Some might say that your battle is not similar to the above issues. That, however, is part of the problem with something that is insidious. Thus, I applaud your battle. Whatever one might think about Vietnam, an author's life should have nothing to do with his works being read, etc.

From Andy Jaysnovitch, 6 Dana Estates Drive, Parlin, NJ   08859:

Once upon a time, you called TMF "the second best fanzine next to TAD."
I joked around a lot about that comment at the time, but I've got to admit it now that TMF *is* probably the second best fanzine next to TAD.   In a lot of ways, it's even better than TAD.
And I think you're right about the L.A. Morse controversy, too.
As for the letter from Otto Penzler, don't forget that TMF is your baby and as editor you should editorialize about whatever strikes your fancy.
It's kind of hard to find the fan in most fanzines these days, but TMF has a most refreshing point of view, and something even rarer these days--an editor who knows what the word means.
Keep up the *great* work!

From Frank Floyd, Rt. 3, Box 535, Berryville, AR   72616:

Like Marvin Lachman, I am in the process of reviewing *To Prove a Villain.*   Unlike Marvin, I read it as soon as I could get my hands on it.
But I find it very difficult to review.   Partly, I feel an overwhelming prejudice in your favor.   Therefore I am taking time to digest and to put my thoughts into a balanced perspective.
Over the years he has written for *The Mystery Fancier*, Marvin Lachman has gotten better and better; he is an astute mystery critic now.   Francis M. Nevins, Jr., is turning out some high class work.

From Herbert Resnicow, 107 Weeks Road, Williston, NY   11596:

[In order for you to understand Herb's letter, you must first read the letter which I wrote to him on 26 December 1986. If you have not yet read Herb's Gold Solution, *you may want to skip the rest of this comment and Herb's letter, since important elements of that novel are discussed. Here's my letter, in it's entirety:*
Just finished reading The Gold Solution, *and I couldn't wait a moment to offer you my congratulations. If your subsequent novels maintain this high level (as I am confident they do), I have a good many pleasurable hours ahead of me as I catch up. Your characterizations are splendid, and your wit pops out in every paragraph.*
I can't, however, resist making a couple of complaints, both of which relate to the elevator. Given your background, I'm probably entirely wrong about the first one, so I'll get it out of the way right now--would an elevator which ran from the cellar to the fourth floor be hydraulic? Now on to the second complaint. On page ten you have Burton say that "If Talbott wanted to carry up more than eighty pounds, or take a visitor to his studio, he would first have to go up alone and release the elevator." As I read that, what we are talking about is a one-person elevator.   But on page fourteen Mrs. Talbott and Dr. Levin both ride up to the top floor at the same time, as do "two men in white." And on page fifteen one of the

two men in white accompanies the stretchered victim down in the elevator. Elsewhere in the book the elevator is used by more than one person at a time—and, of course, the way that the murder was worked required that it be possible for more than one person to use the elevator at the same time. Frankly, Herb, that little mistake (and if it was not a mistake I'd appreciate it if you would explain it to me) really interfered with my concentration throughout the book. If I believed Burton's account, then the elevator was ruled out as a route by which the murderer could have entered the top floor, but I couldn't believe Burton's account since that elevator was carrying pairs of folks up and down throughout the book, except on page ten. But if that part of Burton's account could not be believed, how could I believe any of the rest of it? But how could I not believe it all since Alex and Norma clearly had full faith in Burton's veracity and accuracy. Alas, Herb, it bothered me considerably. But not enough, as I have said, to keep me from enjoying the book tremendously. Thanks for writing it and all the others, which I look forward to reading as soon as possible.]

Thank you for your kind letter. I like to think I have gotten better with each book, so keep plugging away.

Re: your complaints. Please keep sending them on. As I've often said, we writers are like castaways on a desert island who put messages in bottles then cast them into the sea, praying that someone will read what we wrote and, even more, that the messages will be understood. Most fan mail is of the "I just loved your latest" variety. Feels good, but no substance. I hope you don't find any flaws, but you will, you will. A week ago I got a lovely letter from a delightful and intelligent woman I met at the Bouchercon, who told me about a major fault in *The Gold Deadline.* It was psychological rather than technical, but she was absolutely right and I was wrong. I lamely agreed with her, offered the weak excuse that this was my second book and I had not yet developed the incredible skills I now possess, and asked her to keep writing critically and, for the sake of my delicate ego, to balance each found fault with a long, glowing, *specific* description of what especially pleased her and why. I ask the same of you.

There are now problems in having a seven-stop hydraulic elevator (five floors, cellar, sub-cellar). In fact, there are, I understand (I have left the construction business for *good*), buildings with twelve-stop hydraulic elevators. Hydraulics are favored for altering existing small buildings because they require no heavy superstructure on the roof to carry the elevator machinery or, where the machine room can be put into the sub-cellar (which means no stop at that level) no heavy sheave beams and their concomitant loads to be carried by the building's structural supports. The telescoping hydraulic piston which lifts and lowers the elevator need be drilled into the earth (or rock, as is common in Manhattan) a relatively short distance (ten or twelve feet).

I have been putting off answering your second complaint because you are right and have reason to be upset. This failure on the part of the author (who has to be a complete idiot to let a mistake of this order go through) is unforgivable. It made a rational attempt to solve the mystery before the denouement impossible. I have no excuse, but I do have an explanation. A weak one. I assumed, due to my familiarity with the way buildings and their owners work, that it would be obvious that the weighing system would be turned off as soon as R.A. Talbott got to his office, in order to let his wife/maid/visitor/visitor both come up in the elevator at the same time. It would have been easy for me to mention, early on, that RAT automatically disabled that control when he got to his work table. I would have been even easier to leave out all mention of the needless safety feature. Ah, well, we grow too soon old and too late smart.

I believe that I work more tightly in my later books. At least, I try to. (Now I'm going to get a flock of letters from eagle-eyed readers who find even worse boo-boos in my later books.) I'm sorry, I'm sorry. Really.

You may publish all or any part of this letter in *The Mystery Fancier.*

[And so I have. Furthermore, having read your letter closely, I am inclined to think that whatever fault there is lies more in my failure to comprehend than in your failure to explain. But I don't regret having brought up the matter, since it resulted in such an interesting and entertaining letter with which to close out this issue.]

www.ingramcontent.com/pod-product-compliance
Lightning Source LLC
Chambersburg PA
CBHW031616040426
42452CB00006B/546